THE TAKEN-DOWN GOD

Jorie Graham is the author of eleven collections of poetr
Forward Prize for Best Collection in 2012, and *The 1*
Pulitzer Prize in 1996. Her poems have been translated in
French, Spanish, Albanian and Polish. Born in New York i.
Italy and was educated at the Sorbonne, New York Unive.
former director of the Iowa Writers' Workshop in Poetry, she r.

...ie
.. Italian,
.n France and
.versity of Iowa. A
.s at Harvard University.

Also by Jorie Graham from Carcanet Press

The Dream of the Unified Field: Selected Poems 1974–1994
The Errancy
Swarm
Never
Overlord
Sea Change
PLACE

Jorie Graham

THE TAKEN-DOWN GOD

Selected Poems 1997–2008

CARCANET

First published in Great Britain in 2013 by
Carcanet Press Limited
Alliance House
Cross Street
Manchester M2 7AQ

www.carcanet.co.uk

A CIP catalogue record for this book is available from the British Library

ISBN 978 1 84777 194 0

The publisher acknowledges financial assistance from Arts Council England

Supported by
ARTS COUNCIL
ENGLAND

Typeset by XL Publishing Services, Exmouth
Printed and bound in England by SRP Ltd, Exeter

Contents

from

THE ERRANCY

(1997)

THE GUARDIAN ANGEL OF THE LITTLE UTOPIA

Shall I move the flowers again?
Shall I put them further to the left
into the light?
Will that fix it, will that arrange the
thing?
Yellow sky.
Faint cricket in the dried-out bush.
As I approach, my footfall in the leaves
drowns out the cricket-chirping I was
coming close to hear...
Yellow sky with black leaves rearranging it.
Wind rearranging the black leaves in it.
But anyway I am indoors, of course, and this is a pane, here,
and I have arranged the flowers for you
again. Have taken the dead cordless ones, the yellow bits past apogee,
the faded cloth, the pollen-free abandoned marriage-hymn
back out, leaving the few crisp blooms to swagger, winglets, limpid
                                        debris....
Shall I arrange these few remaining flowers?
Shall I rearrange these gossamer efficiencies?
Please don't touch me with your skin.
Please let the thing evaporate.
Please tell me clearly what it is.
The party is so loud downstairs, bristling with souvenirs.
It's a philosophy of life, of course,
drinks fluorescent, whips of syntax in the air
above the heads – how small they seem from here,
the bobbing universal heads, stuffing the void with eloquence,
and also tiny merciless darts
of truth. It's pulled on tight, the air they breathe and rip.
It's like a prize the way it's stretched on tight
over the voices, keeping them intermingling, forcing the breaths to
                                        marry, marry,
cunning little hermeneutic cupola,
dome of occasion in which the thoughts re-

group, the footprints stall and gnaw in tiny ruts,
the napkins wave, are waved, the honeycombing
thoughts are felt to *dialogue,* a form of self-
congratulation, no?, or is it suffering? I'm a bit
dizzy up here rearranging things,
they will come up here soon, and need a setting for their fears,
and loves, an architecture for their evolutionary
morphic needs – what will they *need* if I don't make the place? –
what will they know to miss?, what cry out for, what feel the bitter
                                        restless irritations
for? A bit dizzy from the altitude of everlastingness,
the tireless altitudes of the created place,
in which to make a life – a *liberty* – the hollow, fetishized, and starry
                                        place,
a bit gossamer with dream, a vortex of evaporations,
oh little dream, invisible city, invisible hill
I make here on the upper floors for you –
down there, where you are entertained, where you are passing
time, there's glass and moss on air,
there's the feeling of being numerous, mouths submitting to air, lips
                                        to protocol,
and dreams of sense, tongues, hinges, forceps clicking
in anticipation of… as if the moment, freeze-burned by accuracies-of
could be thawed open into life again
by gladnesses, by rectitude – no, no – by the sinewy efforts at
sincerity – can't you feel it gliding round you,
mutating, yielding the effort-filled phrases of your talk to air,
compounding, stemming them, honeying-open the sheerest
                                        innuendoes till
the rightness seems to root, in the air, in the compact indoor sky,
and the rest, all round, feels like desert, falls away,
and you have the sensation of muscular timeliness,
and you feel the calligraphic in you reach out like a soul
into the midst of others, in conversation,
gloved by desire, into the tiny carnage
of opinions …. So dizzy. Life buzzing beneath me
though my feeling says the hive is gone, queen gone,

4

the continuum continuing beneath, busy, earnest, in conversation. Shall I prepare. Shall I put this further
to the left, shall I move the light, the point-of-view, the shades are
drawn, to cast a glow resembling disappearance, slightly red,
will that fix it, will that make clear the task, the trellised ongoingness
and all these tiny purposes, these parables, this marketplace
of tightening truths?
Oh knit me that am crumpled dust,
the heap is all dispersed. Knit me that *am*. Say *therefore*. Say
philosophy and mean by that the pane.
Let us look out again. The yellow sky.
With black leaves rearranging it....

UNTITLED ONE

A curtain rose. I felt an obligation.
I tried to feel the thing that blossoms in me,
here in my seat, assigned,
the whole world intelligently lit
up there in front of me.
I tried to feel the untitled thing that blossoms in me.
The abnegation that doesn't stutter, not at all, not once.
Or no, that stutters once and once only.
What the days are a rehearsal for: *breathe in, breathe out.*
What the held breath is ventriloquial for,
the eyes quickly shut then scribbled
      back open
again – rasping martyrdom –
the glance once again shouldering the broadcast out there, the loud
          flat broadcast,
the glance ambushed once again by the apparent warmth of the picture.
I blinked. Tomorrow came. Nothing *came true.*
Birds scattered and the minutes clucked, single-file.
Daggering, talkative, the breaths ministered to nothingness.
A tight bond, theirs. An hysterical love. *Never mind* the things said –
those robberies. *I love you,* they said. Or *in a broader sense
this example suggests…* I tried to feel the days go on without me.
Walking in the park: a small tin of shoe-polish
nestled in the grass. From over the trees
the names of people were called out via loudspeaker.
Then there were numbers: the score, incessant coarse ribbon, floated by
          elegantly,
then smeared itself all over the sky…
The small hole inside I'm supposed to love:
I tried to house it – no, I tried to gorge it.
I hovered round it with sentences to magnify the drama.
I cloaked it with waiting. I whispered *don't be afraid*
and petitioned it with rapture – the plumed thing – the cross-dressed
lingering – dramatic – all my thin secrets giddy,

all my whispers free-spending… Tomorrow came.

Slowly it scattered. Then it came again – first fragile, eyes closed,

then, peeling away its cellophane, eyes striating open,

it did it again – and each time so easy; first blurring a bit, then, nearing 5,

the sparrows ascribble, the magnet rising, tomorrow

starting to strip itself clean again of itself. But casually. Tirelessly.

And without innuendo. Just oh so plucky.

Peeling the minutes off, the little white worms.

Quavering up to a strong fine whiteness.

High varnish. Yet noncommittal.

Giving thanks – or so it

seemed – then backing away, unexpurgated, sort of dis-
                              figured.

Then, again, tomorrow came. Never a chorus, only the hero.

And tomorrow, and tomorrow.

One after another, up into the floodlights.

I tried to feel the story grow, name by name,

one at a time. My eyes grew heavy, I could feel my attention slipping.

I tried to shoulder the whole necklace of accidents.

I waited for them all to reappear at the end.

To take a bow. All at once. All together. That I might remember.

THE GUARDIAN ANGEL OF SELF-KNOWLEDGE

How razor-clean was it supposed to become,
the zero at the core of each of these
mingling with leaves as they fork up in wind – bright yellow
                                    distillations of –
uprising evidence of this one world's gigantic
curvature – how clean, how denuded of *their* foliage,
these desperate, aimless ones in twos along the built-up paths,
in ones in corridors, these ones so skillfully grouped up
in liquid clutches of impermanence,
now taking the long way back along the lake,
now in the auditorium beaten upon by wind and then a little
rain. They look in their envelopes.
They look on their paper calendars, under their tongues,
stare at the shadows their bodies cast, stare at the shadows their
                                    folding-chairs cast,
with each glance something like a leaf let loose,
I watch it float, each eyelashed lurching forward, each hoarse
and giddy self-appraisal, I watch them
let it go, each owner standing so stilly now behind his words as they
                                    are given up,
on lunch-break, beside the phone-booth where one's crying
                                    softly now
into the glistening receiver, beside the bookseller, the fruitseller
where one comes right to the warm brink
of a yellow pear – oh from here
it looks so like a dream of shelter –
the way that reaching hand mimics the eye, romancing,
the way it quickens at its root, desiring,
the other one now rooting in a pocket for some change,
and other ones now touching a chin, a lip, an index-finger rough
on a cheek, as if to wipe away a glance – down there – oh how much
                                    must I see – how clean
did they want to become,
shedding each possibility with gusts of self-exposure,
bubbling-up into gesture their quaint notions of perfection,

then letting each thought, each resting-place, get swept away –
because that was *not what I meant – was not at all –*
and since the future isn't real, is just an alarmclock,
where the last domino can finally drop,
wearing a street-address around its medicated neck –
oh that – of course – the wound we cannot medicate –
you know – the room of icons so preserved we move them round to fit
the furniture, opinions nestling in them, down in the folds, the inlays,
opinions and calculations and bits of stardom
right down in there in the grain of the icons,
some truth in there too now, maybe in the form, who can tell,
maybe even some ecstasy, some little monstrosity,
though it doesn't matter,
since we can't tell the difference,
since it's all pre-recorded, or something like that –
who will they be when they get to the bottom of it,
when they've stripped away the retrospect, when they've peeled away the
orphanhood, the shimmering merriments of consolation?
How will they feel the erasures erase them?
Who will they resemble when they're done with resemblance?

THE SCANNING

I.

After the rain there was traffic behind us like a long kiss.
The ramp harrowing its mathematics like a newcomer who likes
                                             the rules –
glint and whir of piloting minds, gripped steering-wheels…
Jacob waiting and the angel *didn't show.*
Meanwhile the stations the scanner glides over, not selecting, hiss –
islands the heat-seekers missed
in the large sea of…. And after lunch
the long-distance starts up pianissimo – wires glinting where the
                                             frontage road
parallels the interstate for a little, narrow, while.
Elsewhere, from the air, something *softens* the scape –
which activity precedes, though doesn't necessarily require,
the carpet-bombing that often follows –
And the bands of our listening scan
the bands of static,
seeking a resting point, asymptotic, listening in the hiss
for the hoarse snagged points where meaning seemingly
accrues: three notes: three silences: intake
of breath: turnstile?: a glint in fog?: what the listener
will wait-into, hoping for a place to
stop… Jacob waited and the angel didn't –

2.

Once off the interstate, we exhausted the tangible.
The plan seemed to dagger forward on its own, towards the horizon-line,
the future its mother-of-pearl cadaver, down there, where the map
                                             continues
onto the next blue page…. *Our* plan.
One must not pretend one knew nothing of it.
One must not pretend one didn't tenderly finger its heavenly style.

10

The skyline itself, bluing now towards evening,
the spidery picture of the plan we tongued up –
unquenchable – where were you? – never-to-be-defined,
a solo first-fruit performance for which the eye
is still intended.... What shall we move with
now that the eye must shut? What shall we sift with
now that the mind must blur? What shall we undress the veilings of
                                        dusk with,
what shall we harvest the nothingness with,
now that the hands must be tucked back in their pockets,
now that the bright shirt of the over-ripe heart
must be taken off and the skin of things restored,
the long-haul restored (where the quicknesses had reigned),
the carpenter arriving as if out of the skyways
with a measure in hand, a sad eye, a vague patience –
the tongue-tied carpenter ready to scribble and strengthen...
Our plan... To get the beauty of it hot.
The angel called out but Jacob, Jacob...

3.

Down by the riverbed I found some geese asleep.
I could see the billboards, but they were across the water.
Maybe two hundred geese – now beginning to stir,
purring and cooing at my walking among them.
Groping their armless way, their underneaths greening.
A slow roiling. As of redundancy. Squirming as they sponge
over the short wet grass – bunchy – the river behind presenting
                            lapidary
                            faithfulness – *plink* –
no common motion in the turbaned brooding,
all shoulder and waddle,
foliage darkening to feathers above their vague iridescence...
A mess of geese. Unperfectable. A mess
of conflicting notions. Something that doesn't have to be
imagined. An end-zone one can have pushed forward to,

here at the end of the path, what the whole freeway led to,
what the whole adventure led to,
galleys, slaves, log-books,
tiny calculations once it got dark enough to see,
what the whole madness led to – the curiosity – viral – here,
like a sign – thick but clear – here at the bottom of the sedge,
the city still glimmering over there in the distance,
but us here, for no reason, where the mass of geese are rousing,
necessity and circumstance quivering in each other's arms,
us in each other's arms, or, no, not really.

4.

The angel was on the telephone.
No, Jacob was on the telephone.
There was no doorway through which to pass.
For either of them. No flaming gateway. No wafer-thin scribble
to *understand*…
Was it really, then, a pastime, the hostile universe?
Was the wrestling a mental color, an architecture of mockery,
a self-portrait of the unmargined thing by the margined thing?
The geese seemed to assemble, the freeway hissed.
Oh to sleep the sleep of those who are alive.…
The brain extended its sugared fingertips.
Itching so to create something new.
Slightly, profoundly, the riverbottom gleamed.

5.

Then *here,* and *here,* a freckling of the light,
as where parts curdle up
to fetch a whole – and the birds lift up –
and from the undulant swagger-stabs of peck and wingflap,
collisions and wobbly runs – out of the manyness –
a molting of the singular,

a frenzied search (upflapping, heavy) for cadence, and then
cadence found, a diagram appearing on the air, at arctic heights,
$$\text{an armoring}$$
the light puts on – stagger of current-flap become unacrobatic industry,
$$\text{no tremble in it,}$$
no echo – below, the freeway lustrous with accurate intention –
above us now, the sky lustrous with the skeleton of the dream of
$$\text{reason – look up! –}$$
Jacob dreamer – the winged volumetrics chiseling out a skull
for the dream –

THINKING

I can't really remember now. The soundless foamed.
A crow hung like a cough to a wire above me. There was a chill.
It was a version of a crow, untitled as such, tightly feathered
in the chafing air. Rain was expected. All round him air
dilated, as if my steady glance on him, cindering at the glance-core where
it held him tightest, swelled and sucked,
while round that core, first a transition, granular – then remembrance of
                                                          thing being
seen – remembrance as it thins-out into matter, almost listless – then,
sorrow – if sorrow could be sterile – and the rest fraying off into all
                                              the directions,
variegated amnesias – lawns, black panes, screens the daylight
thralls into in search of well-edged things…. If I squint, he glints.
The wire he's on wobbly and his grip not firm.
Lifting each forked clawgrip again and again.
Every bit of wind toying with his hive of black balance.
Every now and then a passing car underneath causing a quick rearrangement.
The phonelines from six houses, and the powerlines from three
grouped-up above me – some first-rung of sky – him not comfortable,
nature silted-in to this maximum habitat – *freedom* –
passers-by (woman, dog) vaguely relevant I'd guess though he doesn't
                                              look down,
eyeing all round, disqualifying, disqualifying
all the bits within radius that hold no clue
to whatever is sought, urgent but without hurry,
me still by this hedge now, waiting for his black to blossom,
then wing-thrash where he falls at first against the powerline,
then updraft seized, gravity winnowed, the falling raggedly
reversed, depth suddenly pursued, its invisibility ridged – bless him –
until he is off, hinge by hinge, built of tiny wingtucks, filaments
of flapped-back wind, until the thing (along whose spine
his sentence of black talk, thrashing, wrinkling, dissipates – the history,
                                              the wiring,
shaking, with light –) is born.

THAT GREATER THAN WHICH NOTHING

Even the plenitude is tired of the magnanimous, disciplined,
                              beached eye in
its thrall. Even the accuracy
is tired – the assimilation tired –
of entering the mind.
The reader is tired.
I am so very tired.
Whom will this worry henceforth – radiant striation of hall-light on
                                        pillowcase –
who will receive it –
couch, table, half-open drawer, the granulated dark in it,
the cup, the three glasses – stupefying promises we are supposed to
                                        receive –
The glance? braiding and braiding the many promises of vision?
The glance, however exiled, wanting nonetheless only to come full term
                              into the absolute
orphanhood? *Do you really want to die?*
Do you not maybe want to *sleep it off,* this time, again?
Nothing moves but the cloth as you breathe.
Don't look up at the four corners – the four conquering
                              corners –
for the shape of mercy. It swarms.
It composes gray-eyed walls on which the trapped light plays
                              like fumes off
kerosene – light, light everywhere, beckoning with its epic self-
                              sameness –
all round you, roaming, rough in your shoulders, sparkling,
regrouping – grain by grain, no oases, no conversation –
asking each granulated breath your deep sleep
                    blossoms
to yield to it, to marry up –
and other dimensions – sandy, windy – exact – unincarnate –
                    tireless dimensions –
metamorphic yet unpliant –
now sparkling, sparkling – it's the light, you can't keep it out,

room 363,
its century of wide-eyed wing-work splashing
            hither and thither like graffiti
over the featurelessness – distending – distending the nature of
the erasure – merciless in its lightheartedness

in which the living is forgotten to be living –

STUDIES IN SECRECY

The secret we don't know we're trying to find, the thing *un-*
                                        seen,
is it ironic? is it a sign of anything? – raw
                    vertigo
the suction-point of which we now are trying to feed
                                    our lives
into – the point devoid of ancestry, the bullioned point,
                        so sleek,
dwindling yet increasingly aswarm,
the chittering of manyness in it as it is made to
                            clot
into a thrumming singleness – the secret – the place where the words
                                        twist –
we are looking for it everywhere –
we look on my breast, we try the nipple,
we look in the gaiety of your fingertips, the curriculum
                        of caresses
twisting and windy in the architecture of
                my neck, my
open mouth – we look in your mouth –
we look, quick, into the-day-before-yesterday – we look
                        away –
we look again into your violent mouth,
into the edifice of your whisper, into the dwindling oxygen
                        we eat,
inhaling, exhaling –
we look into the glassy eyes we have between us –
we try not to shift, we stare,
there seems to be an enclosure in there, maybe a struck
                note, an hypothesis,
we look in each other's hair
as in ripe shrubs bearing and withering,
we feel time glide through the room, between our legs,
round through our glance – we think we can look in the walled-up
                        thoughts –

we let our nights get tangled, we try to stare –
if something happens – the phone rings, a cigarette is lit,
maybe a massacre, maybe in spring the curtain
blossoms – gossamer – we look in there –
then we go back to the green-eyed heat, and stare,
beating on the icy film between each thing, knocking, tapping,
                    to see what's happening,
"the wasteland grows; woe to him hiding wastelands
              within" (*The Portable*
Nietzsche – Viking '54 – we look in there),
also look in "Alas, the time is coming when
man will no longer shoot the arrow of his longing
beyond man" – "the string of his bow has forgotten
to whir" – it is a haze – the radio's
         on, the automated
churchbells ring – we start the matter up again, we cry, we finger
the folds – we open our lips – we bite our necks –
don't make me explain, one wing of it is soot, one wing
                of it is blood,
we lick it, we nibble aimlessly, not so much tired as
increasingly ignorant – the minutes barbed now – the
blue streak where we hear a siren louder now,
our shoulders glistening, our backs greasy with hope,
foraging now (we try the book again) (we try putting things
                 in each other
to see how much room) ("the earth has become smaller
            and on it hop
the last men") so that we have to start
saying the words again (the last men live longest) –
I love you I say – poor secret, did you need us?
did you need us to find you? –
(live longest – *we have invented happiness,* they say) –
I love you, you say, rising among the motes, the spores –
and *forever and forever* like a sleeve we slide the hissing secret in –
the golden-headed, the upthrown – have invented *happiness* say the
    last men –
and blink.

LE MANTEAU DE PASCAL

I have put on my great coat it is cold.

It is an outer garment.

Coarse, woolen.

Of unknown origin.

       ◦ş

It has a fine inner lining but it is
as an exterior that you see it – a grace.

       ◦ş

I have a coat I am wearing. It is a fine admixture.
The woman who threw the threads in the two directions, headlong,
has made, skillfully, something dark true,
as the evening calls the birds up into
the branches of the shaven hedgerows,
to twitter bodily
a makeshift coat – the boxelder cut back stringently by the owner
that more might grow next year, and thicker, you know –
the birds tucked gestures on the inner branches –
and space in the heart,
not shade-giving, not
chronological… Oh transformer, logic, where are you here in this fold,
my name being called out now but back, behind,
in the upper world….

       ◦ş

I have a coat I am wearing I was told to wear it.
Someone knelt down each morning to button it up.
I looked at their face, down low, near me.
What is *longing?* what is a *star?*
Watched each button a peapod getting tucked back in.
Watched harm with its planeloads folded up in the sleeves.
Watched grappling hooks trawl through the late-night waters.
Watched bands of stations scan unable to ascertain.
There are fingers, friend, that never grow sluggish.
They crawl up the coat and don't miss an eyehole.
Glinting in kitchenlight.
Supervised by the traffic god.
Hissed at by grassblades that wire-up, outside,
their stirring rhetoric – this is your land, this is my *my* –

                    ·5

You do understand, don't you, by looking?
The coat, which is itself a ramification, a city,
floats vulnerably above another city, ours,
the *city on the hill* (only with hill gone),
floats in illustration
of what was once believed, and thus was visible –
(all things believed are visible) –
floats a Jacob's ladder with hovering empty arms, an open throat,
a place where a heart may beat if it wishes,
pockets that hang awaiting the sandy whirr of a small secret,
folds where the legs could be, with their kneeling mechanism,
the floating fatigue of an after-dinner herald,
not guilty of any treason towards life except fatigue,
a skillfully-cut coat, without chronology,
filled with the sensation of being suddenly completed –
as then it is, abruptly, the last stitch laid in, the knot bit off –
hung there in Gravity, as if its innermost desire,
numberless the awaitings flickering around it,
the other created things also floating but not of the same order, no,

20

not like this form, built so perfectly to mantle the body,
the neck like a vase awaiting its cut flower,
a skirting barely visible where the tucks indicate
the mild loss of bearing in the small of the back,
the grammar, so strict, of the two exact shoulders –
and the law of the shouldering –
and the chill allowed to skitter-up through,
and those crucial spots where the fit cannot be perfect –
oh skirted loosening aswarm with lessenings,
with the mild pallors of unaccomplishment,
flaps night-air collects in,
folds… But the night does not annul its belief in,
the night preserves its love for, this one narrowing of infinity,
that floats up into the royal starpocked blue its ripped, distracted
                                        supervisor –
this coat awaiting recollection,
this coat awaiting the fleeting moment, the true moment, the hill, the
                                        vision of the hill,
and then the moment when the prize is lost, and the erotic tinglings
                            of the dream of reason
are left to linger mildly in the weave of the fabric,
the wool gabardine mix, with its grammatical weave,
never never destined to lose its elasticity,
its openness to abandonment,
its willingness to be disturbed.

July 11… Oaks: the organization of this tree is difficult. Speaking
generally no doubt the determining planes are concentric, a system of
brief contiguous and continuous tangents, whereas those of the cedar
wd. roughly be called horizontals and those of the beech radiating but
modified by droop and by a screw-set towards jutting points. But beyond
this since the normal growth of the boughs is radiating there is a system of
spoke-wise clubs of green – sleeve-pieces. And since the end shoots curl
and carry young scanty leaf-stars these clubs are tapered, and I have seen
also pieces in profile with chiselled outlines, the blocks thus made

detached and lessening towards the end. However the knot-star is the chief thing: it is whorled, worked round, and this is what keeps up the illusion of the tree. Oaks differ much, and much turns on the broadness of the leaves, the narrower giving the crisped and starry and catherine-wheel forms, the broader the flat-pieced mailed or chard-covered ones, in wh. it is possible to see composition in dips, etc. But I shall study them further. It was this night I believe but possibly the next that I saw clearly the impossibility of staying in the Church of England.

⋯

How many coats do you think it will take?

The coat was a great-coat.

The Emperor's coat was.

How many coats do you think it will take?

The undercoat is dry. What we now want is?

The sky can analyze the coat because of the rips in it.

The sky shivers through the coat because of the rips in it.

The rips in the sky ripen through the rips in the coat.

There is no quarrel.

⋯

I take off my coat and carry it.

⋯

There is no emergency.

⋅⊱

I only made that up.

⋅⊱

Behind everything the sound of something dripping

The sound of something: I will vanish, others will come here, what is that?

The canvas flapping in the wind like the first notes of our absence

An origin is not an action though it occurs at the very start

Desire goes travelling into the total dark of another's soul
looking for where it breaks off

I was a hard thing to undo

⋅⊱

The life of a customer

What came on the paper plate

overheard nearby

an impermanence   of structure

watching the lip-reading

had loved but couldn't now recognize

⋅⊱

What are the objects, then, that man should consider most important?

What sort of a question is that he asks them.

The eye only discovers the visible slowly.

It floats before us asking to be worn,

offering "we must think about objects at the very moment
when all their meaning is abandoning them"

and "the title provides a protection from significance"

and "we are responsible for the universe."

❧

I have put on my doubting, my wager, it is cold.
It is an outer garment, or, conversely, a natural covering,
so coarse and woolen, also of unknown origin,
a barely apprehensible dilution of evening into
an outer garment, or, conversely, a natural covering,
to twitter bodily a makeshift coat,
that more might grow next year, and thicker, you know,
not shade-giving, not chronological,
my name being called out now but from out back, behind,
an outer garment, so coarse and woolen,
also of unknown origin, not shade-giving, not chronological,
each harm with its planeloads folded up in the sleeves,
you do understand, don't you, by looking?
the Jacob's ladder with its floating arms its open throat,
that more might grow next year, and thicker, you know,
filled with the sensation of being suddenly completed,
the other created things also floating but not of the same order,
not shade-giving, not chronological,
you do understand, don't you, by looking?
a neck like a vase awaiting its cut flower,

24

filled with the sensation of being suddenly completed,
the moment the prize is lost, the erotic tingling,
the wool-gabardine mix, its grammatical weave
– you do understand, don't you, by looking? –
never never destined to lose its elasticity,
it was this night I believe but possibly the next
I saw clearly the impossibility of staying
filled with the sensation of being suddenly completed,
also of unknown origin, not shade-giving, not chronological
since the normal growth of boughs is radiating
a system of spoke-wise clubs of green – sleeve pieces –
never never destined to lose its elasticity
my name being called out now but back, behind,
hissing how many coats do you think it will take
"or try with eyesight to divide" (there is no quarrel)
behind everything the sound of something dripping
a system of spoke-wise clubs of green – sleeve-pieces –
filled with the sensation of suddenly being completed
the wool gabardine mix, the grammatical weave,
the never-never-to-lose-its-elasticity: my name
flapping in the wind like the first note of my absence
hissing how many coats do you think it will take
are you a test case is it an emergency
flapping in the wind the first note of something
overheard nearby an impermanence of structure
watching the lip-reading, there is no quarrel,
I will vanish, others will come here, what is that,
never never to lose the sensation of suddenly being
completed in the wind – the first note of our quarrel –
it was this night I believe or possibly the next
filled with the sensation of being suddenly completed,
I will vanish, others will come here, what is that now
floating in the air before us with stars a test case
that I saw clearly the impossibility of staying

RECOVERED FROM THE STORM

I went out afterwards to see.
Wide silvery hypotheses of memorizing waters.
In them – so deeply – the incomplete pictures.
Twigs, seeds, nuts, limbs scattered over the streets,
distemper's trophies gathering round our footfalls.
I looked at them carefully, wide awake in that monologue.
Some branches thrown down in the middle of things.
Cars not yet venturing. Dusk so blue in its black.
And whole bushes torn from some too-thin origin.
And drowned heads of things strewn wildly through
our singular, tender, green,
        clarifications…
Am I supposed to put them back together –
these limbs, their leaves, the tiny suctioned twig-end joints – ?
these branches shoved deep into my silky glance – ?
these maples' outtakes streaked over the lawn – their thorns, their blithe
footnotes…? And the trellis cracked from the weight of the freefall?
And the boxelder standing like an overburdened juggler –
so laden now he cannot remember
the sugary spinnings, the bright fingerings of…
Oh limpid puddles with your ditties of fate…
There's a shovel by the window.
There's contagion by the gutter.
There's a cartoon upstairs where the children are hidden.
So this is the wingbeat of the underneathly, ticking –
this iridescent brokenness, this wet stunted nothingness –
busy with its hollows – browsing abstractly with its catastrophic wingtips
the tops of our world, ripping pleatings of molecule,
unjoining the slantings, the slippery wrinklings we don't even grasp
        the icily free *made-nature* of yet?
Why are we here in this silly moonlight?
What is the mind meant to tender among splinters?
What was it, exactly, was meant to be *shored?*
Whose dolled-up sorceries *against confusion* now?
The children are upstairs, we will keep them tucked in –

as long as we can, as long as you'll let us.
I hear your pitch. How containment is coughing,
under the leafbits, against the asphalt.
How the new piles of kindling are mossily giggling
        their kerosene cadenza
all long the block in the riddled updrafts.
I pick up and drag one large limb from the path.

OF THE EVER-CHANGING AGITATION IN THE AIR

The man held his hands to his heart as he danced.
He slacked and swirled.
The doorways of the little city
blurred. Something
leaked out,
kindling the doorframes up,
making each entranceway
less true.
And darkness gathered
although it does not fall.... And the little dance,
swinging this human all down the alleyway,
nervous little theme pushing itself along,
braiding, rehearsing,
constantly incomplete so turning and tacking —
oh what is there to finish? — his robes made rustic by the reddish swirl,
which grows darker towards the end of the avenue of course,
one hand on his chest,
one flung out to the side as he dances, taps, sings,
on his scuttling toes, now humming a little,
now closing his eyes as he twirls, growing smaller,
why does the sun rise? remember me always dear for I will
return —
liberty spooring in the evening air,
into which the lilacs open, the skirts uplift,
liberty and the blood-eye careening gently over the giant earth,
and the cat in the doorway who does not mistake the world,
eyeing the spots where the birds must eventually land —

from

SWARM

(2000)

from THE REFORMATION JOURNAL (1)

The wisdom I have heretofore trusted was cowardice, the leaper.

★

I am not lying. There is no lying in me,

★

I surrender myself like the sinking ship,

★

a burning wreck from which the depths will get theirs when the heights
have gotten theirs.

★

My throat is an open grave. I hide my face.

★

I have reduced all to lower case.

I have crossed out passages.

I have severely trimmed and cleared.

★

Locations are omitted.

Uncertain readings are inserted silently.

Abbreviations silently expanded.

★

A "he" referring to God may be capitalized
or not.

★

(is crying now)   show me

★

is crying now   (what's wrong)

★

in a strange tree   of atoms   of

★

too few   *more*   no wonder

★

Give me the glassy ripeness

                                        ★

Give me the glassy ripeness in failure
                                        ★

Give me the atom laying its question at the bottom of nature
                                        ★

Send word   Clear fields
                                        ★

Make formal event   Walk
                                        ★

                         Turn back
                                        ★

Reduce all to lower case   Have reduced all
                                        ★

Cross out passages   Have inserted silently
                                        ★

is there a name for?
                                        ★

glassy ripeness
                                        ★

in failure
                                        ★

born and raised
                                        ★

and you?
                                        ★

(go back)   (need more)
                                        ★

having lived it   leaves it possible
                                        ★

fear   lamentation   shame   ruin   believe me
                                        ★

explain   given to
                                        ★

explain   born of
                                        ★

Absence is odious   to God
                                        ★

I'm asking

$\star$

Unseen unseen   the treasure unperceived

$\star$

Unless you compare   the treasure may be lost

$\star$

Oh my beloved   I'm asking

$\star$

More atoms, more days, the noise of the sparrows, of the universals

$\star$

Yet colder here now than in

$\star$

the atom still there at the bottom of nature

$\star$

that we be founded on infinite smallness

$\star$

"which occasions incorruption or immortality"

$\star$

(incorruption because already as little as it can be)

$\star$

(escape square, wasted square, safety square, hopeless square)

"to all except anguish the mind soon adjusts"

$\star$

have reduced, have trimmed, have cleared, have omitted

$\star$

have   abbreviations   silently   expanded

$\star$

to what   avail

$\star$

explain   asks to be followed
explain   remains to be seen

THE VEIL

Exile   Angle of vision.

So steep   the representation.

Desperate   Polite.

A fourth wall   A sixth act.

Centuries lean up into its weave, shudder, go out.

Tongue caresses its entireties.

Look closely for the adjusting of wings,

the knife removed from breast, the noose from

neck,

the acid slippers of eternity being tried on each new foot,

and the patience of understudies, the curtain that cannot rise or fall

over the depth of field. Oh love.

What war did we hope for?

What sleep?

Couldn't the orchestral die down a while—

burning bushes, moving vans—little plazas—eyes of the lion?

What if the rear-view were to open up?

The whole unseeable back where the blood flows off,

34

drying so quickly,

us broom in hand trying to sweep the front porch off,

every now and then looking up to see how soon.

How soon?

The clouds haul off across.

We tidy up. (*I see*).

War then tidying-up then war. (*I see*).

Shovel the rubble to the roadside. (*gesturing*)

Let the carts loaded with interpreters
                    get by.

It is years.   Goodnight says

the heaven at our backs. (*points*)

Greatness   is sleepy.

Oh my stringed-thing, throat,

when was it I first took this pencil and wrote out

this emptiness you hold now to your ear—

listen: the other place is in it still.

The drawers are full.

Nothing scares off.

I knock on the front

whispering open up, forgive us,

can you grow any more silent?

The windows glint to me

re the straight paths of the right hand,

the refusal that anything be measured
                              or judged,

up here in the shiny
          democracy,

the so-called cup of bitterness,

the so-called train

picking up speed, the so-called

sublime it flatly aims for—

Are we alone? I can never think of you
                    without smiling.

Underneath (Sibylline)

As if we could tell

if we'd been abandoned.

The battle took so long that soon between the enemies
                                    the bonds
emerged.

Also slowly extinguishing: the sounds of birds, the barking
of dogs.

Planets howl.

Musics rise and fall below the battle sounds.

And you, one being with two parts:

there exists only one instant in which

you can both gain and lose your life.

Remain seated says the voice-over.

(Shouldn't the red light blink?)

Corridor   Curiosity

Appointment   Time

Gods defeated or perhaps   in fact—

(*I can smell it, can't you?*)—

What would you like, someone asked long ago,

ancient, I'm ancient the one in line before me screams.

I haven't given up on you darling, the hum replies.

I'm planting a wildfire

in your head,

I'm watching I'm remembering,

even though you're dead, you know, you're old tricks—

And this office is swarming with talent.

But what would you *like*?

To stay in your skin?

You've got all of us turning inside-out for you,

but what is it you're suffering from?—

blinking on and off

in the margin,

the free race,

where I goes without saying,

where it begs the question?

Oh bend.

Open your hiding places.

Burn all the letters.

Look in the ashes with both hands.

Finger in there for any bits intact.

              Wrist-deep

in the fine grains, so cold,

feel further round for fragments,

for any last unburnt

piece of

the crashing of mind,

or any promises (so parched) come down through the sentences
                                 to breathe,

pushing the few bits back to the tiny fire,
              the struck match,

and worrying, and keeping each fragment lit to the very end

by turning it

to every side   every last side—

Look you have to lift the match to it again

because this syllable   is still intact.

MIDDLE DISTANCE

This is certain.

Dream has no friends.

Bottom is there but depth conceals it.

Centuries cannot see us.

Here, in liberty.

(enter others)

What are these eyes for?

What are these hands for?

I have been listening. A long time (looks around)

The "frontier labyrinth" (gestures)

All the people in history (gestures further)

The heart in my throat (spotlight on wilderness)

Then their eyes were opened and they knew and it
vanished from sight.

This is certain.

Dream

will not vector

is illegitimate

hangs over us huge dry wings

suffers with us   grows worse

is not identical with awareness

often lies under the cathedral floor

ought to spare us

oh surely it ought to spare us

entertaining brevity like a sweet curiosity

always the wings opening and closing at a
                              constant rate

as if nothing were happening

never beckoning or imploring why do we
                              stay

has a sharpness, is raven-dark,
      perhaps weak eyesight

is humble   is authentic

(though of course in the inaudible)

usually in bed at night the wings
                    tie down

you can hear them like a growing
                    of the dark

although all of it of course stays the same

(none of the letters have been saved)

This is certain: inwardgoingness of the
soul

that won't lie down

vague gods

no possible restoration of order

bright city held at the hinge of
the wings

remembered touch   weary hands

flame snapping the air in

its one body of bright singularity

dust on the fire becoming fire

and how we shall be obedient

dust on the fire

on the seeming

apple in hand

in the wake of the wings

("speechless sorrowing of Nature")

(you will get lost   you will be left)

bending over looking for the trinket lost

(most quiet heaven)

pale light of the reasons

soul walking in circles

weary scribe

Fly I say, reins in the
            one hand
you now dislodging centuries
            need me
by offering yours suddenly   to free

Wheel without faces on it

Happened   to be

PRAYER

(after Hölderlin)

Should we not speak of you?
Should you ring in us   as an idle caprice

pressed into   service,
should we not, you deed rampaging destiny, furious,

pressing voice into service,
as if the hurling of hot arrows,

pressing the good into your service,
making it play for you?

And yet you will veil our eyes
that we not perish.

Hard burden. Names and names.
Likewise the river.

I called you once and thought you once.
You travel down to me on your allotted paths,

a light embrace, miraculously omnipresent.

Underneath (Calypso)

1

Sing to me   of time and time again

being driven   off course

to face   another audience

bewitching   craving to hold

him   back

I apologize   to coincidence

I apologize   to necessity

Let happiness try to receive the dead

Apologize   to the war I steal him from

You must forgive   this veil

It's like a laughing   time and again

I wanted to be   everything

I know nothing can justify   the veil

Be brave   Let it descend

2

Why should the exile   return home?

Era?   Period?

Discover: Calypso has shuffled the deck.

Has veiled the early with the late.

Has veiled sequence.

Remembering violent   as it must be,

and it all now middle-time.   Sleep, love.

What must be   inferred under

the blemished   mantling   shimmers.

How else to keep you.

I apologize to history.

I covered the story with all these words.

Overgrown with eyes.

3

The stress and drag of looking.   Look.

Shuffled the deck   to veil phenomena, yes.

Strike me says each thing.

Resurrect me   in *my*   flesh.

Do not pass through me.

4

Look how our mouths   are bared.

And those, still strapped in their seats, the others.

I am held to myself   by force.

No voyage   home

over blossoming's   broad back.

Forced down instead   into the stalk.

Let your soul slip through   radiance

Let not radiance cling to you   Push through

5

How we walk the aisle: in flames.

Frothing time back   into its corner.

In anguish here   under the veil.

Going broken   before some altar.

Two Days (5/2/97—5/3/97)

Full moon; lays his hand
onto her throat, into his mouth
takes her whole ear.

Noon: this pen hovers
over this empty page. One is
free to forget.

Noon. The gate fills to
its edges with the two sides of
opening. Move.

Noon. Regardless of
the gate, buds open all around,
stare at each other.

Noon: evaporation is taking
place.

Full moon: your body before me
a nameless hill.

Full moon: seeing, being-seen;
the cold lies in us all night long.

In one spot most especially.

I am not seeking altitude.

Noon: we push until
like a third party

matter rages between us.

Noon: pushes us
into the midst to where
Spring stops.

Noon: pushes us
to where a crown emerges and begins to lower
all round our bodies
tiny rips of buds.

Noon: then even the buds push out
into this emptiness.

Noon. The only heaven plays and leaps.

Dusk, with its downslope,
a bride, and one above her
all shivering of mind.

Late dusk: a communication
between what exists and what
is visible (that shore) (who knows

what can be said)—

Full moon;
lays his hand onto her throat, into his mouth
takes her whole ear.

THE SWARM
(Todi, 1996)

I wanted you to listen to the bells,
holding the phone out the one small window
to where I thought
the ringing was—

Vespers scavenging the evening air,
headset fisted against the huge dissolving

where I stare at the tiny holes in the receiver's transatlantic opening
to see evening-light and then churchbells

send their regrets, slithering, in—
in there a white flame charged with duplication—.
I had you try to listen, bending down into the mouthpiece to whisper, hard,

can you hear them (two petals fall and then the   is wholly
changed) (yes) (and then another yes like a vertebrate enchaining)
yes yes yes yes

We were somebody. A boat stills on a harbor and for a while no one
appears,
not on deck, not on shore,
only a few birds glancing round,

then—before a single face appears—something
                            announces itself
like a piece of the whole blueness broken off and thrown down,
a roughness inserted,

yes,
the infinite variety of having once been,
of being, of coming to life, right there in the thin air, a debris re-
assembling, a blue transparent bit of paper flapping in also-blue air,

boundaries being squeezed out of the blue, out of the inside of the blue,
human eyes
held shut,

and then the whisking-open of the lash—the *be thou, be thou*—

—*a boat stills in a harbor and for a while no one*
appears—a sunny day, a crisp Aegean blue,
easy things—a keel, a sail—

why should you fear?—
me holding my arm out into the crisp December air—
beige cord and then the plastic parenthetical opening wherein I

have you—you without eyes or arms or body now—listen to

the long ocean between us

—the plastic cooling now—this tiny geometric swarm of
openings sending to you

no parts of me you've touched, no places where you've

gone—

Two petals fall—hear it?—moon, are you not coming soon?—two fall *from* THE REFORMATION JOURNAL (2)

It was during one of these times that
I felt the midst of its suffering,

the presence of its suffering,
like a smile on a beloved face though not exactly

No one   no messenger sent   no image either

One is left to live purely by analogy

By an extreme effort of concentration

Looking just ahead to what appears to be
a pile of wretched flesh in a corner mildly brown

A bit further up the factory   the enormous debt

The sunlight very still on everything animate and in-
                                    animate
making a sound like *it is enough that you exist*

Is it not?

Is not the desire now to lose all personal will?

Come evil, my first person is hidden.

Look, I can rip it off (the pile in the
                    corner)

(once it beheld wondrous things)

(that is to say the things that are underneath)

And the narration

which relates the things

(but they must   be true)

The path of thought also now too bright

So that its edges cut

So that I'm writing this in the cold

keeping the parts from finding the whole again

page after page, unstitched, speaking for sand

Look I push the book off my desk

into the flood

"Let him be prepared to give the poison twice or
            even thrice if necessary"

As when feeling you watch my sleeping body

Underneath (13)

needed   explanation

because of the mystic nature   of the theory

and our reliance   on collective belief

I could not visualize the end

the tools that paved the way broke

the body the foundation the exact copy of the real

our surfaces were covered

our surfaces are all covered

actual hands appear but then there is writing

in the cave   we were deeply impressed

as in addicted to results

oh and dedication training   the idea of loss of life

in our work we call this emotion

how a poem enters into the world

there is nothing wrong with the instrument

as here I would raise my voice but

the human being and the world cannot be equated

aside from the question of whether or not we are alone

and other approaches to nothingness

(the term "subject")(the term "only")

also *opinion* and *annihilation*

(the body's minutest sensation of time)

(the world, it is true, has not yet been destroyed)

intensification   void

we are amazed

uselessness is the last form love takes

so liquid till the forgone conclusion

here we are, the forgone conclusion

so many messages transmitted they will never acquire meaning

do you remember   my love my archive

touch me (here)

give birth to   a single idea

touch where it does not lead to war

show me   exact spot

climb the stairs

lie on the bed

have faith

nerves wearing only moonlight lie down

lie still patrol yr cage

be a phenomenon

at the bottom below the word

intention, lick past it

rip   years

find the burning matter

love allows it (I think)

push past the freedom (smoke)

push past   intelligence (smoke)

whelm   sprawl

(favorite city)   (god's tiny voices)

hand over mouth

let light arrive

let the past strike us and go

drift   undo

if it please the dawn

lean down

say   hurt   undo

in your mouth be pleased

where does it say

where does it say

this is the mother tongue

there is in my mouth a ladder

climb down

presence of world

impassable   gap

pass

I am beside myself

you are inside me   as history

We exist   Meet me

from

NEVER

(2002)

PRAYER

Over a dock railing, I watch the minnows, thousands, swirl
themselves, each a minuscule muscle, but also, without the
way to *create* current, making of their unison (turning, re-
                            infolding,
entering and exiting their own unison in unison) making of themselves a
visual current, one that cannot freight or sway by
minutest fractions the water's downdrafts and upswirls, the
dockside cycles of finally-arriving boat-wakes, there where
they hit deeper resistance, water that seems to burst into
itself (it has those layers), a real current though mostly
invisible sending into the visible (minnows) arrowing
                    motion that forces change—
this is freedom. This is the force of faith. Nobody gets
what they want. Never again are you the same. The longing
is to be pure. What you get is to be changed. More and more by
each glistening minute, through which infinity threads itself,
also oblivion, of course, the aftershocks of something
at sea. Here, hands full of sand, letting it sift through
in the wind, I look in and say take this, this is
what I have saved, take this, hurry. And if I listen
now? Listen, I was not saying anything. It was only
something I did. I could not choose words. I am free to go.
I cannot of course come back. Not to this. Never.
It is a ghost posed on my lips. Here: never.

In/Silence

I try to hold my lie in mind.
My thinking one thing while feeling another.
My being forced. Because the truth
is a thing one is not permitted to *say*.
That it is reserved for silence,
a buttress in silence's flyings, its motions
always away from source; that it is reserved for *going* too, for a deeply
artifactual spidery form, and how it can, gleaming,
yet looking still like mere open air, mere light,
catch in its syntax the necessary sacrifice.
Oh whatever that might be. How for song
I looked today long and hard at a singing bird,
small as my hand, inches from me, seeming
to puff out and hold something within, something that
                                        makes
wind ruffle his exterior more—watched
him lift and twist a beak sunlight made burnt-silver
as he tossed it back—not so much to let
anything *out* but more to carve and then to place firmly in the
                                        listening space
                                        around him
a piece of inwardness: no visible
passaging-through: no inner complication and release:
no passage from an inner place—a mechanism
of strings, bone, hollow
chamber—no native immaterial quiver time turns material—
then towards [by mechanisms ancient and invisible] expression,
and the tragic of all upward motion—
then it all lost in the going aloft with the as yet
                        unsung—then
the betrayal (into the clear morning air)
of the source of happiness into mere (sung) happiness.
Although there is between the two, just at the break

of silentness, a hovering, almost a penitent
                    hesitation, an
intake, naked, before any dazzling release
of the unfree into the seeming free, and it seems
it goes elsewhere, and the near (the engine) overruns
into the truly free. This till the last stars be counted?
This plus the mind's insistent coming back and coming back?
This up against that coming back. The death of
uncertainty. The song that falls upon the listener's *eye*,
that seeks the sleek minimum of the meaningless *made*.
Here in the morning light. In matter's massive/muscular/venerable holding-in
of all this flow. Next door the roses flow.
Blood in the hand that reaches for them flows.

WOODS

O stubborn appetite: *I*, then *I*,
loping through the poem. Shall I do that again?
Can we put our finger on it?
These lines have my breathing in them, yes.
Also my body was here. Why try to disguise it.
In this morning of my year
that will never be given back.
Also those who will not give it back. Whoever they
                                              may be.
How quietly they do their job
over this page. How can I know when it's the
case—oh swagger of dwelling in place, in voice—
surely one of us understands the importance.
Understands? Shall I wave a "finished" copy at you
whispering do you wish to come for lunch.
Nor do I want to dwell on this.
I cannot, actually, dwell on this.
There is no home. One can stand out here
and gesture wildly, yes. One can say "finished"
and look *into* the woods, as I do now, here,
but also casting my eye out
to see (although that was yesterday)(in through the alleyways
of trees) the slantings of morninglight
(speckling)(golden) laying in
these foliate patternings, this goldfinch, this
suddenly dipping through and rising to sit very still
on top of the nearest pine, big coin, puffed-out,
little hops and hopes when he turns, sometimes
                                  entering into
full sun—becoming yellowest then—these line
                        endings
branching out too only so far
hoping for the light of another's gaze to pan them,
as the gaze pans for gold in day, a day sometimes overcast,
                                        but what

would the almost-gold (so that I can't
say "golden") bird be but your eye?
Do not harm him. I can bring him back,
and the way he hopped, turning, on the topmost spike
of the pine—how many minutes
ago was it I said "golden"—and does he still linger there
turning chest into and out of the story, hot singular,
not able to shed light off himself yet so
                              full of my
                         glance—me
running on something that cripples me—
do not harm him, do not touch him, don't probe
with the ghost your mind this future as it lays itself out
here, right over the day, straight from the font, and yes
I *am* afraid, and yes my fear is
flicking now from limb to limb, swooping once completely out of
sight—oh flickering long corridor—then
                              back,
the whole wind-sluiced avenued continuum taking
my eye around in it—who could ever hold so many
thoughts in mind—him back now, back, my fear,
and my mind gathering wildly up to still itself on him.

DUSK SHORE PRAYER

The creeping revelation of shoreline.
The under-shadowed paisleys scripting wave-edge down-
                                                  slope
on the barest inclination, sun making of each
                    milelong wave-retreat
a golden translucent forward downgoing,
golden sentences writ on clearest moving waters,
moving their meaninglessness on (not *in*) the moving of the
                                                  waters
(which feels tugged)(the rows of scripting
        [even though it's a trick] adamant with
self-unfolding)(wanting the eye to catch and take
dominant final-hold, feel the thickest rope of
                    waterlipped
                    scripting
to be a producing of a thing that speaks [to whom
one does not know, but a true speech])—to believe this truly,
                    not in metaphor—
to put it in the blank in which one *sees*,
and then into the blank in which one *is*,
to separate *I am* from *I have being* from *I am
apart*. And not to want to *be*. And never to be
emptied by the wound of meaning.
The gash of likeness. The stump interpretation.
Spelled from the living world. Grown sharper by
this sighting. As sun goes down. Until it glimmers in
the tiny darkness and the human will comes to the end.
Having it go before one's looking goes. The summer
at one's back. The path back barely findable.

GULLS

Those neck-pointing out full bodylength and calling
outwards over the breaking waves.
Those standing in waves and letting them come and
go over them.
Those gathering head-down and over some one
thing.
Those still out there where motion is
primarily a pulsing from underneath
and the forward-motion so slight they lay
their stillness on its swelling and falling
and let themselves swell, fall...
Sometimes the whole flock rising and running just
as the last film of darkness rises
leaving behind, also rising and falling in
tiny upliftings,
almost a mile of white underfeathers, up-turned, white spines
gliding over the wet
sand, in gusts, being blown down towards
the unified inrolling awayness
of white. All things turning white through
breaking. The long red pointing of lowering sun
going down on (but also streaking in towards) whoever
might be standing at the point-of-view place
from which this watching. This watching being risen
from: as glance: along the red
blurring and swaying water-path:
to the singular redness: the glance a
being-everywhere-risen-from: everywhere
cawing, mewing, cries where a
single bird lifts heavily
just at shoreline, rip where
its wing-tips (both) lap
backwash, feet still in
the wave-drag of it, to coast
on top of its own shadow and then down to not
landing.

*

Also just under the wave a thickening where
sun breaks into two red circles upon the
                    carried frothing—
white and roiling, yes, yet unbreakably red—red pushed (slicked) under
                    each wave (tucked) and, although breaking, always
                    one—(as if from the back-end-of-distance red)—
and that *one* flowing to here to
slap the red it carries in glisten-sheets
up onto shore and (also as if *onto*)
my feet.

*

[Or onto my feet, then into my eyes] where red turns into "sun" again.
So then it's sun in surf-breaking water: incircling, smearing: mind not
knowing if it's still "wave," breaking on
itself, small glider, or if it's "amidst" (red turning feathery)
or rather "over" (the laciness of foambreak) or just *what*—(among
the line of also smearingly reddening terns floating out now
on the feathery backedge of foambroken
looking)—*it is*.

*

The wind swallows my words one
                    by
one. The words leaping too, over their own
                              staying.
Oceanward too, as if being taken
                    away
into splash—my clutch of
                    words
swaying and stemming from my
              saying, no

68

echo. No stopping on the temporarily exposed and drying rock
                                                out there
to rub or rest where nothing else
                        grows.
And truly swift over the sands.
As if most afraid of being re-
                        peated.
Preferring to be dissolved to
                designation,
backglancing stirrings,
wedged-in between unsaying and
                        forgetting—
what an enterprise—spoken out by
                me as if
to *still* some last place, place becoming even as I speak
                                unspeakable—
"we shall have early fruit
this year" one of the shades along the way
                        calls out,
and "from the beginning" (yet further on). Words: always face-down:
listening falling upon them (as if from above):
flinging itself upon them: them open and attached
                        so hard to
                        what they carry:
the only evidence in them of having
                        been.
And yet how they want to see behind themselves—
as if there were something back there, always behind,
feeling them rush a bit and crane to see beneath themselves—
twisting on their stems—as if there were a sun
back there they need, as if it's a betrayal,
this single forward-facing: reference: dream of: admission: re
semblance—you are not alone:
slowly in the listener the prisoners emerge:
slowly in you reader they stand like madmen facing into the wind:
nowhere is there any trace of blood
spilled in the service of law, or love, or for the sake of honor,
or for some other reason.

EBBTIDE

I am a frequency, current flies through. One has
                              to ride
                              the spine.
No peace [of mind][of heart], among the other
frequencies. How often and how hard are answerings.
The surf, receding, leaves successive
hem-line trims of barely raised institching sand—
bridal-wreath puckerings—
glassy (this side), packed smooth (that).
Making one's way one sees the changes.
What took place before one
                    looked.
Snakeskin of darker sands in with the light.
Slightly more raised and wider alligator-skins.
Crabtracks' wild unfocusings around firm holes.
The single tubefish, dead, long as a snake, half-snout,
rolled over and over as the waves pick up, return, return
less often, go away. For a while he is incandescent
white, then blue, deep green, then white again, until he's
                              left, half-turned,
eyes sandy till one wave, come back
this far as if in error, cleans him off.
Greenish with rising/falling weed-debris, shoremist
fingering long streaks of sun.
Graphed beachlength on the scallop-edged lapping retreat:
                    christmas-ornament red shrimp
punctually along the highs of each
upskirting arc—prongs upright,
stiff. Swift ticks of sunlight count them
                    out.
Who has enough? A little distance
                    back
two vultures feeding on a pelican. Later, claws and beak
float in the brack. Foam-bits lace-up the edge
of the retreat. Something feels like it's not

coming back. In the tidepool
sand-grains advance along a long
walled avenue, in ranks—at the conjunction of
                    two rocks, algae
signaling the entry point—(swarming but
                    swaying in
unison, without advancing) (waiting for
                    some arrival)
(the channel of them quickening)(the large espousal)(light
beginning now to *touch* what had been only
                    underwater story)—
until the gleaming flow of particles is finally
                    set down, is
                    stilled: the grains
drop down and mat, silt in, begin to dry: the wandering tribe is
                                        gone, the
city's gone, the waiting gone. The individual grains
are not discernible. I'm squatting so I hear
sand sucking water in. Gravity. Glistening.
I take a stick and run it through
the corridor of wilderness.
It fills a bit with water the first time. Is self-erased.
The second time it does not fill. It leaves a
                    mark where
my stick ran. I make
another (cursive) mark. How easily it bends to cursive, snakes towards
                                        thought.
                                    Looking back

I see the birds eating the bird. The other way my
gaze can barely reach shore-break.
The (little) weight of the stick in my hand. The meditation
place demands. My frequency. This hand, this
sugar-stalk. The cane-fields in the back of us,
the length of tubefish back there too. And
if I write my name. And how mist rounds the headland
                                    till the sea
is gone. One feels word should be sent us

from some source. It is all
roar and cry and suck and snap. The pebbles on the
pebbles roll. One feels one has in custody
what one cannot care for for long. Too much is
asked. Nothing is coming back the way it was.
But one can wait for the next hem, next bride,
next oscillation, comedy. Done, the birds fly
off. I can see through the trees,
through the cane grove, palm grove, out far enough into
                              the clearing where
the spine of the picked-clean story shines.

EVOLUTION

One's nakedness is very slow.
One calls to it, one wastes one's sympathy.
Comparison, too, is very slow.
Where is the past?
I sense that we should keep this coming.
Something like joy rivulets along the sand.
I insists that we "go in." We go in.
One cannot keep all of it. What is enough
of it. And *keep?*—I am being swept away—
what is *keep?* A waking good.
Visibility blocking the view.
Although we associate the manifest with kindness.
The way it goes where it goes, slight downslope.
Like the word "suddenly," the incline it causes.
Also the eye's wild joy sucked down the slope the minutes wave
                                        by wave

pack down and slick.
The journey—some journey—visits one.
The journey—some journey—visits me.
Then this downslope once again.
And how it makes what happens
            always more heavily
laden, this self only able to sink (albeit also lifting
                        as in a
sudden draught) into the future. *Our* future. Where everyone
is patient. Where all the sentences come to complete themselves.
Where what wants to be human still won't show
                        its face.

EVOLUTION

How old are you?
As old as until now.
Under the kelp-bed razorclams turning to find
                                    purchase.
Young things shooting first-times and retaining
                                    precedence.
Razors digging backwards and down,
spurting spittle-bits of sea
to equalize descent.
Do you believe that after you die some part of you
                                    lives on?
Do you pray in hope of reward?
Do you agree or disagree with the following
                                    statement:
it bothers me my life did not turn out as I
                                    expected.
Also there are people on the beach.
And wind accepted by waterfilm.
Look: acceptance has a shape.
And fate—is it accepted by waterfilm?
And how we must promise things.
Do you pray in hope of reward.
Do you pray without hope of reward.
What is it has been gone a long time?
How long is the slightest chance?
Everything in sunlight
improvising backwards,
scratching phrases in a rapid jitter,
where the mind above it begins, ends, tries to get up
                                    and move
towards or away from.
You'll feel the so-called music strut hard against
                                    the downsuck.
Also someone's shadow going to purchase a beverage.

Also everything in sunlight trying to become bodied by something
                                                    else,
the whole retreating ocean laying
microscopic and also slightly larger fiercely-lit
kelp in streaks of action—
long sentences with branchlike off-widths indicating
                        acceleration brought forth
and left-off, phrases of gigantic backing-off
                from a previously
held shore,
            rivulets of sand left visible in raised inscription
whitening where moistened—questionlike—algebraic—
regarding the long leave-taking—
We are ourselves walking to the right.
The noon hour is itself always a firstness
                    of something.
Also, elsewhere, who is hungry?
How small are they? How? I step on parts of
faces, only parts. A whole face, what is that? From here
it seems hard to make out, also a very empty
thing. Like the border of a nationstate.
Being comes into this, idles,
over the interminable logic of
manyness, the demand that *something exist.*
Bending to look close, a
spiking-up and forth of burrowings,
channelings, a turning, a re-turning on
itself where the broad
nouns of large clamshells
flayed open by gulls lie
in punctuating sunlit stillness
on top of a thing which but for
their stillness and expulsion
has no top. The seagulls
hurrying, dragging and retrieving. Also
pecking in place and dropping and
lifting. Sometimes stepping backwards in order to

drag and loosen. Also the drag of the slantline
downtilted towards ocean's sucking further still of
streams of water towards
itself. Of course the future
wasn't there before at all.
This all first time and then again first
                              time.
I feel reproach. Eyes closed I touch my face.
My hand hovers like the very question of my face
                              over my face.
G says, breathing beside me, that firstness is not, in any case,
a characteristic of experience.
He speaks of the long chain back
to the beginning of "the world" (as he calls it) and then, at last,
                              to the great *no*
beginning. I feel the *no* begin.
Subsequence hums tinily all round me,
erasing my tracks. Oh bright/morning. This
                              morning.
Look: what looks like retreating is not exactly so.
Sunlight makes of exactness an issue.
No issuing *forth* of matter
because of sunlight. But sun's
up-sucking also at work. And how
it seems to have weight,
pushing the originally pillowy kelp-beds
down, flattening them where they
give up water, unthickening their
pastures as the tunneling-away from
that gigantic drying drives
the almost-imperceptible downwards:
first glitter then more unchangeable shine slowly being
forced into the vast top of the
beachwide beds. Drying out and
hardening, the beds force light
                              back.
Back across what resides inside.

White closed-in part of gazing-out.
Bothered by the ease of touch.
As if one should open out and spill, again.
Sound in the sun now muted
(is there an inherent good)
as the ruffling back-roar recedes
(is there inherent good in people)—
Sound becoming particular and pricked
with syncopations of singularities—
peeps, insucks, snaps—where light is
                              in domain.
What good is my silence for, what would it hold
                         inside, keeping it free?
Sing says the folding water on stiller water—
one running through where the other's breaking. Sing me
something (the sound of the low wave-breaking)
(the tuning-down where it deposits life-matter on
the uphill of shore)(also the multiplicity
of deepenings and coverings where whiteness rises as a
                              manyness)
(as the wave breaks over its own breaking)
(to rip in unison)(onto its backslide)—
of something sing, and singing, disagree.

from

OVERLORD

(2005)

OTHER

For a long time I used to love the word *now*. I murmured its
tiniest of songs to myself as a child when alone. *Now now now
now* I sang, not much knowing where we were. Until, before I knew it,
it put forth its liquid melody, and time, shimmering, began to flow
nearly inaudible, alongside the crickets if it was summer, alongside the penumbral
clock if it was the kitchen, alongside the tapping of the wintered lilac's branches on the
violet-shadowed

walls that held the garden,
if it was wind. Where were we, in fact? *Now now* the adults used to say
meaning pay attention, meaning the thing at hand, the crucial thing, has these
slippery sides: this *now* its one slope, this *now* its
other. The thing itself, the essential thing, is in between. Don't blink. Don't
miss it. Pay attention. It's a bullet.
All those years, before I became lost, I lived a different life.
One where you can go back. I thought each new
now, new

note, plucked from the as-yet-unpronounced, covered up a footstep
of the retreating God.

Where was it just before, I wondered, as it moved away in concentric circles
from the place the finger had triggered. *Tap tap* drummed my mother's hand
without her knowing on the kitchen table
in the dim end of afternoon. To keep away waiting. There is no
waiting. There will never be tomorrow. Nonetheless you do suddenly fall asleep, and then,
there it is again, when just as suddenly your eyes open, it floods in, and you
are full, and the song begins. One day
I woke up, I was

sick, in bed, my first time, since beginning, since beginning
school, since the becoming of my self.
I looked for the notes but walls slid in. A weight
descended. I was waiting. The first time. What age could I have been?
The house gave forth its ticking and tapping. One-time sounds occurred—a shutter
snapped,

a heavy clink where keys were dropped, the sweet dry
clack where a pinecone hits

gravel below. A mourning dove. Once. Then after a while, again, once.
What else could be inside me? That's when I heard
what makes me break this silence and speak to you this way.
I heard my name, as always, called out into the classroom as the schoolday began.
PEPPER, Jorie. I sat up. I knew what space it floated into, everyone waiting.
I heard it said the second time into the grayish morninglight
over the rows and rows of chairs, the gleaming fullness of them, empty, as children stood.
There was nothing I could do. I saw it as I heard it—"absent"—
said out into the room. Heard the silence that followed it.
Sitting up, I looked about. The tree beyond the windowpane flowed out to its bark.
It ticked out its being to its leaftips, down into its roots. *It could not be*

                          absent. The blue

cup on the dresser, its tiny blue stream, crabapples in bloom, one bird sitting on
the handrail of the bridge—what of it could ever retreat,
leaving only part of itself present?—or the clouds—on cup, in sky—or the tasseled

                                    fringe of

curtain, door, wicker chair with rose-pattern pillow, saffron lampshade with cream-
brocaded border…I don't know if I cried out,
but they came running up to see what was wrong.
This is what is wrong: we, only we, the humans, can retreat from ourselves and

                              not be

                              altogether here.

We can be part full, only part, and not die. We can be in and out of here, now,
at once, and not die. The little song, the little river, has banks. We can pull up

                  and sit on the banks. We can pull back

from the being of our bodies, we can live in a
portion of them, we can be absent, no one can tell.

DAWN DAY ONE
(Dec 21 '03)

A gunshot. The second, but the first I heard.
Then the walls of the room, streaked with first light, shot
                                       into place.
Then, only then, did my eyes open.
We come about first, into waking, as an *us*, I
think. Sometime between the first and second instant
there is still the current that carries one in
and deposits one in singleness. The body's weight is
a beaching. Back behind, or underneath: infinity
or something which has no consequence. Then consequence, which
feels like walls and the uprighting of self one has to do
in them, then the step one has to take once roused, and how it
puts one back on the walking-path one stepped off of
last night. Zeno reasoned we would
never get there. Reason in fact never gets there.
But we step back onto the path each time.
How long have you been yours, are you tired, are you
in a hurry, are you sitting down, is that stillness
still your pathway which you enter
                      now only with
your mind—which keeps on stepping mind you—
until it doesn't and the stopping
                    happens again.
Are your eyes shut? I put cream on my lids
and rub it in. I feel my eyes in there under the skin.
How impersonal are they, these hardnesses, barely
attached, in their loosely protected sacks.
Tony tells me how, in the lab, they cast an image
—a cross in this case—onto the gaze of a monkey then
                                   "sacrifice
the monkey" and how, when examined, the neurons in the
                              visual cortex
actually form the imprint of

the cross. It would have been, the cross (except under very
                    unusual circumstances), erased
by the next image. Hence the need for
sacrifice. Of what is it made, I ask. Of cells, of *active*
cells, he says. Is it imprinted, I ask. No. It
would have disappeared and been replaced except
the creature was stilled. I like it they
use the word *stilled*. Then the back
of the cave in there with its cross of cells. Which will
dissolve as the "next instant." Some arguments
continue this way ad infinitum. And
infinitum *is* one path, but you can't
really get onto its promenade, its boardwalk, by
speculation. "Therefore" is another way to walk,
therefore the fast Achilles can never best the slow
tortoise. Zeno inferred yet another way.
And yes, now space and time can be subdivided
infinitely many times. But isn't this sad?
By now hasn't a sadness crept in?
I put my hands over both my eyes and lie
still. I think. The paradox says that you can never leave
the room in which you are right now. First walk
half the distance to the door, then half again, and so on. These eyes,
under my hands, I looked at in the mirror yesterday.
Everything of course was silver, my skin, my gaze,
and then the eyes, held in
                    their lids.
Looked hard into that room.
Looked everywhere, all the way to the back. The
                              back
                            tells me
I have to come back here, here to the front, there is
no further I can go. One takes smaller and smaller steps
according to Zeno to try to leave the room. If you return now
to the glass, you can look *at* your eyes. After a short
time, very short if you hold fast, don't blink, just stare,
you will be looking at *an other*. A silver one. I promise

you, go do it now, you will see it, it is not you.
It is more exactly not-you than anyone you've
ever seen. Keep staring. Even Achilles must take
smaller and smaller steps. Even so he can never win.
Before Zeno there was Pythagoras. Before Pythagoras humans
did not understand—that is the verb that is used—that results
had to be proved. That there is an edifice
you can build, level upon level, from first principles,
using axioms, using logic. Finally you have a house
which houses you. Now look at you.
Are you an entire system of logic and truth?
Are you a pathway with no body ever really on it?
Are you shatterable if you took your fist now to
this face that looks at you as you hold to your stare?
Here. You are at the beginning of something. At the exact
beginning. Ok. This is awakening
number two in here, in this poem. Then there are
these: me: you: you *there*. I'm actually staring up at
you, you know, right here, right from the pool of this page.
Don't worry where else I am, I am here. Don't
worry if I'm still alive, you are.

SOLDATENFRIEDHOF

(German Cemetery, La Cambe, Normandy, 2003,
Computer Terminal)

"To find a fallen person," it says, "push green key."
Fill in name, last name, first name, I put in
Klein. 210 Kleins in the Soldatenfriedhof.
I scroll. Klein stays the same.
The first name changes, rank, row, plot.
No. The graveyard changes too. At 88 Klein's in
Colleville (US graveyard). At 93 he's in the British one (Bayeux).
Have you found your fallen person says the program
when I go back to the home page. No slot for
nationality. None for religion. Just date of
                                    birth,
then rank, row, plot, and field come forth. I'm staring at
                                    the soundless
screen. Keys very large for easy use.
Back through the doorway there's the
field. 21,222 German soldiers. Some named, some not.
Inside the office now a wide face looking up.
When is the last time a new man was found, I ask.
Here it is full, he says, people now go to Saint André.
So there are no new bodies being found?
Oh no. No, no. Just last month eight—
here look, pulling a red file from a stack.
Look—and it's open—here, you'll see.
A name, a question mark, a print of teeth of which two
(lost after death) marked "lost after death." A plastic
baggie holds an oval metal tag, almost
illegible, now placed into
my hand. The other baggie he snaps open: here:
a button: we mostly tell them from the buttons:
this was a paratrooper: you can see from
the size, the color of the casing. The sleeve
of something other than time, I think,

slides open to reveal, nested, as in a pod, this seed, hard, dark, how does he
                                                        make out its

identity—a paratrooper—a German one—each people's
buttons different—if it's a German, we get called—if he is ours
we begin work—whatever clothing still exists—part of
                                        a boot,

a lace, can get you back
the person—a metal clip—the stitching of a kind of
cloth. There were so many kinds of fiber then. Then
as much soil as we can get—bone-fragments when there are—
how fast flesh turns to soil again—that is why clothing is
                                        so good.

Where there are teeth too it is good—
we will be able to notify the family.
There is great peace in knowing your person is found.
Mostly in Spring when the land is plowed.
Sometimes when they widen roads.
Many were put in with the apple trees.
One feels, from the way they are placed, the burying
was filled with kindness. I don't really know why, but it is
so. I turn the oval in my hand. Soil on it still, inside the chiseled number-
                                                        group, deeper

in the 3's and 8's, so that it's harder to make out the whole.
The boy is 17 he says.
What if he hadn't been found.
What if he is now found.
What does he re-enter.
Saint André de Champigny will receive
some earth, jaw, teeth, buttons, dog-tag, an
insignia, hair, bones of most of one
right hand. When more than one have been found
together, the official of the graves registration department
—this man with soft large hands holding the folder out—
portions out enough human remains
to make up as many people as possible.
The possible person: a tooth is enough. *Anything*
                                will do

really, he says looking up, almost inaudibly.
With whom is he pleading.
Behind him now the field where in 1947 American bodies, and parts-of, put here
                                        temporarily,
were dug up and moved for the final time
to their last resting place, to the American Normandy War Memorial—
and these available German parts and wholes pulled from their
holding grounds and placed in openings Americans
                            released.
Forgive me says the man still in his seat,
I have been rude, I did not mean (gets up)
my name is _____, here is my card.
May I hold the button a moment longer?
You from under the apple orchard,
you still not found in my field,
and the mole hacking through,
and the rabbits at dawn eating,
and the bird I cannot identify,
you, meaninglessness,
speak out—what do you hate—what do you hate—

UPON EMERGENCE

Have I that to which to devote my
self? Have I devotion? The shoes, the
clothes? The drowning of appetites, as the chariots
were drowned? I sit at the very edge
of the garden, paying out my attention.
The moving and moving of the mottled interminable
forms—the deepness in the unseen, the
different deepnesses in the lisping way the gaze
takes time to alight. Nothing is solid as itself—
that too. A style to the visible world which is—yes like
death—but also like a spume, or the way music seems to formulate
words—a style which I can feel slip free of
point of view and gaze, the artificer mind
making explicit what is not—as in the version of a place
                                  inside a place. Is it a
future that I see? Right here, just underneath this rock I
lift—brood of tiny helmets going everywhere towards defeat—is it
sunlight laying itself hard
on the geranium leaves—which it also
fattens—an existent thing, the sun, yes, and yet, if so, *where*
does it exist? The fine hairs on the geranium leaves stand up
and catch the light. If you bend close you'll see the
future there—do you remember? "Do you remember" is that what devotion says? Do not forget to
remember. I feel, inside, a fantastic pressing of blood against
this skin. I hold my open hands up, here,
before my face, I listen hard to them.
Clouds press. The passings of their shadows press
onto each palm. There is no underneath.
It is all souvenir.
The bird that was just feeding here
is now appearing in my mind. The blood
inside me now must take it round and round. Hardly changed,
it bends and pecks at the last bits of seed below
the lavender. Riding on the blood in me,

its wings spread out. And also bloody, yes, the grass
of mind, bright red its stalks. Also glints on its claws, its
wingtips rising up, above the streams—of me? in me?—
borne round and round by my sticky devotion here, my *thinking* it….
So this is the source of evil? Of course I know
how small it is. But what lies buried at the core
of this holding-in-mind, this final place in which we are
compelled to bury it? We live in time. It is a
holiday. All round it timelessness which will begin again,
yet still, for now, sticks to *one* time like remnant rain
after the place is solidly in place under fresh sun.
Concerning the gods I have no means.
But from this path what is it must be
seen, what must be thought and spoken of—from this,
what is it that is taken from the visible—
what is it that cannot be given back
in *any* form—which burns off—without
residue—just by coming into contact with
the verb of human inwardness? How helpless they are—
both sides—can the gods really know?—the
ineffable pain, amazement, thronging drift
of accident whereby freedom of world, of
subject, are forced to give way? Oh
"path of inquiry"! All of it unable to die
or kill. Also unable to stay calmly underneath, or *in* any arrival place—no hell, even,
no hell.…I know it is only the visible world.
But nothing is small enough to escape us.
Can I devote myself to setting it free?
Where, where is it free? Before I think it,
what is its state? And if I summon it
to mind, if I begin to summon it? Unbearable
                              tyranny. Tiny
monster picking up the reins of my eyes.
The chariots of the sun "says" the tiniest god (definition).
Beyond whispers the hillside, the paragraph
break, the insuck of breath before this
rest. *Where is your brother* hisses the page.

90

LITTLE EXERCISE

The screen is full of voices, all of them holding their tongues.
Certain things have to be "undergone," yes.
To come to a greater state of consciousness, yes.

Let the face show itself through the screen.
Let the organizing eyes show themselves.
Let them float to the surface of this shine and glow there.

The world now being killed by its children. Also its guests.

An oracle?—a sniper, a child beater, a dying parent in the house,
a soil so overfed it cannot hold a root system in place?
Look—the slightest wind undoes the young crop.

Are we "beyond salvation"? Will you not speak?
Such a large absence—shall it not compel the largest presence?
Can we not break the wall?
And can it please *not be a mirror* lord?

PRAYING *(Attempt of May 9 '03)*

I don't know where to start. I don't think my face
in my hands is right. Please don't let us destroy
Your world. No *the* world. I know I know nothing. I know I
can't use you like this. It feels better if I'm on
my knees, if my eyes are pressed shut so I can see
the other things, the tiniest ones. Which can still escape
us. Am I human. Please show me mercy. No please show
a way. If I look up all the possibility that you
might be there goes away. I need to be curled up this
way, face pressed, knees pulled up tight. I know
there are other ways, less protected, more expressive of
surrender. But here I can feel the whole crushing
emptiness on my back. Especially on my shoulders.
I thought just now how that emptiness could be my wings.
That you were there, maybe, laughing. That the room above me,
here, before dawn, its two windows black, this
pillow pressed down hard against me, how it, how all of it,
made up the wings. There is a reason I
have to go fast. Have to try to slide into
something I can feel the beginning of. Right
here in my pushed-down face. Right
where eyes are pressed
so sleep doesn't go there anymore.
And the mirror—well that is another way if you wish. If you
look in for a very long time. But here, I did this other thing
again. (Here)(I write the open parenthesis, press my face,
try again, then lift, close)(then this clause to explain)
(to whom?)(always wanting to be forgiven)(not seen)(no)—See,
it is already being lost here, the channel is filling
in, these words—ah—these, these—
how I don't want *them* to be the problem too, there are
so many other obstacles, can't these be just a part of
my body, look (put my head down again)(am
working in total dark)(maybe this will not be
legible)—my ears covered to go further—maybe

if I had begun otherwise, maybe if I had
been taught to believe in You, I needed evidence,
others seem not to need it, they do not seem to me
graced, but yesterday when I asked Don he said yes, he
                              was sure, yes,
everything was His plan, so it is a lapse of faith
to worry, you will have noted I cannot say "Your
plan," and now, as if dawn were creeping in, the
feeling of the reader is coming in, the one towards which
this tilts, like the plant I watched a long time yesterday the
head of, and then the stem itself,
to see if it turned towards the light as the light arrived,
I would say it did, very slightly, and I
                    could not *see it*,
though I never lifted my gaze, and tried very hard to blink only
when physically impossible not to, and yes, yes, in the end it
was in a different direction, I had marked where we started
so I knew for sure, although of course I know nothing, I could
begin this story anywhere, maybe I will open my
eyes now, although I have gotten nowhere and will
                      find myself
still just here, in the middle of my exactly given years, on
my knees naked in my room before dawn, the pillow
wet of course but what of it, nothing nothing comes of it,
                          out there where the
garbage truck will begin any second now, where I
can feel the whitening reefs (which
I have only read about)(if that means anything)(yes/no) under there where
                              they are,
the waters filtering through them, the pH wrong, the
terrible bleaching occurring, the temperature, what
is a few degrees, how fine are we supposed
to be, I am your instrument if you would only use me, a
degree a fraction of a degree in the beautiful thin
water, flowing through, finding as it is meant to *every*
hollow, and going in, carrying its devastation in, but looking so
simple, and a blue I have never seen, with light still in its

body as light is in mine here I believe, yes,
light a chemical analysis would reveal,
something partaking of the same photons
in this pillow, this paint on the wall, this wall,
which if I open my eyes will be five inches from my face,
which (the coral reefs having caverns) I try to go into—
because I can make myself very small is that a gift from you,
I think it might be one of the great gifts, that I can *make*
myself very small and go in, in from this room, down into the
fibrous crenellations of the reef, which if you look close are formed
by one node clipping onto an other, and then
the rounding-up as the damage occurs, as the weight is lost, now the coral
$$\text{in with the}$$
trucks, pipeknock kicking in, it is beginning
again—oh—when I open my eyes I see two white lines,
vertical, incandescent, I will keep all the knowledge
away I think, I try to think, I will keep
the knowing away, the lines seem to come out of nowhere,
they do not descend nor do they rise,
just gleam side by side in the small piece of glance
my two eyes hold in their close-up
vision. There is a flood. There are these two lines.
Then the sun moves up a notch, though still in the invisible, and I see, I see it is the 12-ounce glass, its body
illumined twice, white strokes where the very first
light has entered, here, I look again, it seems to gleam, it
gleams, it is the empty glass.

PRAYING *(Attempt of June 14 '03)*

This morning before dawn no stars I try again.
I want to be saved but from what. Researchers in California have
discovered a broken heart causes as much distress
in the pain center of the brain as physical injury.
The news was outside the door on the landing. I
squatted to it then came back in. Resume my
position. Knees tight, face pressed. There seems to be
a canyon. No light in it, yet it's there, but then
nothing. *Waste* comes
in, I know they are
burying our waste, that it will last hundreds of millions
of years in the mountain, that they are trying to cover it with signs they
do not know how to develop in
a language that will still communicate in that far
future saying don't open this, this is lethal beyond
measure, back away, go away, close the lid, close
the door. The canyons where my face lies full weight on the platter
of my hands have ridges and go forward only to
the buried waste. If there is beauty growing on those
flanks, beauty in detail—furred underside
of small desert leaves comes to mind but only as idea—
the sage twiggy stuff with its blue flowers—the succulent
floor plants that rise—the hundreds of crossing mucus-tracks on the walls where the
                                              snails have been
guiding the first light
down their slick avenues to some core—all of it *just in*
mind not on my closed face trying
so hard to let the thing that can save us in—if
there is beauty it is missing in its manyness is only there
in form I am trying to be honest I am not relying on
chance any more I am trying to take matters
into my own hands. Hand heart head.
Brain pain center sleep. I try to
remember. Something that *was* once is not graspable
from here. Here is all here. Is the problem. Have

tucked the body away. Am all alone on this
floor. In a city in America. To make a
sacrifice. Of what. Save my beloveds. Save my
child. Save her right now. Destroy this carpeting these
windows the walls take the whole of what is wrong
in payment from us. Let me fall through the air.
Save the will to live, save the constituent part of
the human. No. What is constituent. Oh
save my child, my only child.
The more I press down onto the rug the more we move up the
canyon. In Mycenae we moved up this canyon too,
up, up through the city to the throne room at the top.
The columns still standing. The view of two oceans and over two
ranges. Where the King and his retinue are receiving the news. Here. The
poet ushered in. To sing of what has happened. Right here.
On this floor. The voice telling its story. Long, slow, in detail. All of them
waiting. Listening for the terrible outcome. In detail. The opening
of the singer at the throat. The still bodies of the
listeners, high on this outpost, 3,000 years ago, the house of
Agamemnon, the opening of the future. There. Right through the open
mouth of the singer. What happened, what
is to come. And the stillness surrounding them when it is done,
the song. And the singer still. And the chalices empty.
Dawn about to open it all up again. Dawn about to
move it from inside the mind back out. Light almost visible
on the far hills. Oh who will hear this. When it comes it will be time only for
action. Keep us in the telling I say face to the floor.
Keep us in the story. Do not force us back into the hell
of action, we only know how to kill. Once we stop singing we
only know how to get up and stride out of the room and begin
to choose, this from that, this from that, this from that,—and the pain,
the pain sliding into the folds of the brain and lodging.

Look, the steps move us up through the dark, I can hear them
even though I can't see them, we are moving further up,
this that this that and the pain sliding all along,
sliding into the fine crevices on the side walls of this brain we are

traveling up, and the pain lodging, and the pain finding the spot of
unforgetting,

as in here I am, here I am.

SPOKEN FROM THE HEDGEROWS

I was Floyd West (1st Division) I was born in Portia Arkansas Feb 6
1919 We went through Reykjavik Iceland through the North Atlantic through the
                                                    wolf packs
That was 1942 I was Don Whitsitt I flew a B-26 medium bomber
Number 131657 called the Mississippi Mudcat I was a member of

The 387th Bomb Group and then later the 559th Bomb
Squadron. Picked up the Mudcat in Mt. Clemens Michigan
Flew over our whole group four squadrons sixteen planes each
from Hunter Field at Savannah Georgia then to Langley Field at

Norfolk Virginia from there to Grenier Field at Manchester New Hampshire
In each place stayed a day or two
From Grenier went on to port of embarkation
which was Presque Isle, Maine, then started across, first to Goose Bay, Labrador,

then to Bluie West One, Greenland, then over the cap to
Mick's Field, Iceland. Made landfall at Stornoway, Scotland, from there
down to Prestwick, north London, finally Station 162 at Chipping
Ongar. My name was Dan, 392nd Squadron of the 367th Fighter Group

March 21 boarded the *Duchess of Bedford* in NY,
an old English freighter which had been converted
to bring over the load of German prisoners, whom we replaced

going back to England. Slept below decks in hammocks.
April 3rd arrived at Scotland, and, following a beautiful trip through
the country, arrived at Stoney Cross, ten miles from the Channel—

it was a beautiful moonlit night. I was known as Bob. I was in
D Company. My number was 20364227. I was born Feb 3,
1925, Bristol, Tennessee. We embarked on the HMS

Queen Mary, stripped, painted dull gray, hammocks installed with
troops sleeping in shifts. The *Queen* was capable of making twenty-eight knots
and therefore traveled unescorted, since it could outrun any

sub. Walter, given name, 29th Division. We crossed on the *Queen Mary*. The swimming pool was covered over, that's where most of us slept.
My name was Alan, Alan Anderson, 467th Anti-Aircraft Artillery. I was given

birth November 1, 1917, Winchester, Wisconsin. They took us to
Fort Dix for England. We took the northern route in the extreme rough sea of
January. It was thought that this would confuse the

German subs. It didn't exactly work that way.
A convoy ahead of us by a few days was hit, many ships sank.
I saw the bodies of so many sailors and soldiers floating by us

with all the other debris and ice on the water. The name given me
was John, born September 13, '24, in Chattanooga, but raised
in Jacksonville. I was a person, graduated high school in '42,

crossed over on the *Ile de France,* a five-decker, ten thousand on board.
They loaded over twenty on the *Queen Mary*
there on the other side of the pier. My name was Ralph, Second Class Pharmacist's Mate,
July 4 received orders to Norfolk. There's no describing

crossing the Atlantic in winter. We couldn't stay in our bunks
without being strapped in and fastened to metal pipes on
each side. We had one meal a day. My name, Robert, was put to me

in Atchison, Kansas, United States, August 15, 1916, year of the

Lord we used to figure on, there, in the 149th Engineer Combat Battalion,
which arrived Liverpool, England, January 8 1944. It rained every day.
From there we were taken to the town of Paignton. The authorities

would go down the road, and the truck would stop, and they'd say
"All right, three of you out here" and they'd march you to a house and say to
                                                                    the owner,
"all right, these are your Americans. They are going to be staying with you."

IMPRESSIONISM

(near St. Laurent sur Mer)

1.

Under her bonnet the silent little girl
in a white frock whose puffed-up sleeves sputter
                                in the little
wind, whose also-white pinafore slaps its looping back-bow
this way and that against the landscape, stands
                                very still,
on a small, arcing, quasi-ornamental bridge over the inlet streaming
                                between dunes and land.
Sun shines down hard.
Everything seems to want to shout something out.
Beyond her, on that side, dune and tall dune grasses
                                juggling long winds all one way
at any given once,
                    made silvery by every mile-long bend.
She's leaning on the wooden rail. Her frock is jagged in its
                                private wind
of starch and straightenings and cleanliness. Her hair
is held by tiny yellow bows.

2.

Downstream blue herons, two, wade in and fish.
Each beak catches the light a little differently.
Also, once, the foot uplifts in the isosceles
of just a single wading-step—half-interrupted now, as if mid-thought.
                                Look how it's held
as the eye discerns, among the currents, the half-truth that can
                                be caught.

3.

I feel these are the tablets of the law.
Midsummer, noon, grass, sand, surf, cloth.
Rectitude of birds. In-
candescent pinafore where she leans out over the
                                        railing now.
The parked cars gleam. The streamlet gleams.
What is it one would listen past to hear?
Hands in my pockets I think of the holy tablets
again, trying to look everywhere at once.
What more am I supposed to do.
The bottom of things is neither life nor death.
The bottom is something else.

4.

As if a tree could siphon all its swollen fruit
back in, down into its limbs, dry up the
                            tiny opening
where manifestation slipped out—
taking it all back in—until it disappears—until
that's it: the empty tree with all inside it still—
versus this branching-out before me of *difference,* all
                               brilliantly lit, out-
                            reaching, variegating,
feeding a massive hunger.
The heron is full of hunger.
The miles of one-thought-driven grasses full of
                                  hunger.
Although not in this register.

5.

I feel there is only one question.
Everywhere the shine covering the *through*
through which hunger must move.
And gladly. It must be done gladly or it
                                   will not
serve. And yes there is surplus—
but on the surface (untouchable) and in the
                                   narrow
(inaudible) we are slaves, ferrying the hunger back and
                                             forth.

6.

From the railing, down into the streambed,
a yellow string hangs from the fist of the
                                   child—
crayon-yellow—fuzzy—with tiny filaments light lets us
                                       see wind in.
It is repeated on the surface, then where it enters,
                                   breaks.
Wind throbs sky, dress, grasses, about, but
the string's held taut by something underneath, so taut that very
close you'd hear the thrumming it is forced to make.
Perfect vertical! Calm fills me as I reach the
                                   child.
What's on your string, I ask, arms full—towels, shoes, basket and
                                             my book.
Where are the others is something that I also think.
Also how full my head is of the wind,
papery, stripping my face away—hot dry woodplanks
                                       where my feet
are placed. Let it come on.
If I stand still I see
the shadow of the string on wood

grow shorter as it's drawn back up into
its source. Soon *something* will be here. I feel
consumer confidence: I laugh
out loud. A little wind.
Birdcheeping in the tall grass now.

7.

Swollen, thick, pin-cushioned-up with fat and slack-dead open
                                                    pores,
the bleached-out jumbo turkey-leg and thigh draws up
knotted to this yellow string—eleven crabs attached, all feeding
                                        wildly on their
                                        catch, clacking
their armors onto each other, claws embedded—pulled-up
                            by the yolk-
                            yellow force
onto the dock and crushed, each, at the head by the child's hammer
                                        taken to them
one by one—fast—only one scrambling across the bridge today
                            to get away—
the leg/thigh leaking all over the fading grayed-out planks,
the full-moon catch of crabs picked up claw-end by many
hands that seem to suddenly materialize
out of the nowhere to which I am
                    now sent.
There's no way back believe me.
I'm writing you from there.

PRAYING *(Attempt of April 19 '04)*

If I could shout but I must not shout.
The girl standing in my doorway yesterday weeping.
In her right hand an updated report on global warming.
An intelligent girl, with broad eyes and a strong
wide back. What am I supposed to tell her?
Outside the trees seem healthy to me, and the street is filled
with human busyness. Oh street. Built to conduct
all of our errands and appointments and even some secret running to
assignation. I feel now all the streets holding us up
as if they had a kind of patient willingness—no hopelessness—
just holding till it is time to be opened and undone.
The map of my city plays itself over my eyes, a piece
of vibrant lacework—of which I have seen the first
11th-century sample—which took the eyesight of the 12-year-old
assigned it. Lace where the knots of the individual
                                        strands
are too small for the human eye as we know it to see.
Has the human eye changed. The eye doctor asks me
if it is more like dust or soil, the matter my eye splays
against the empty walls. More like dust. Then it's ok.
It's really my own blood I see.
It will disintegrate, just not right away. When it goes
from dust to soil I should come back. Writing this
has been a very long detour I know.
No one likes to lie or be lied to.
Do I ask the help of the four walls and the hard
                        soil-covering street
to answer the student still standing here?
The answers are unknown, but the possible truths
forbidden. Because we cannot ask another to live
without hope. Above—above all this—I have lived out my
life. Indulgent with hope. Given freedom to wonder.
To mull, speculate, praise.
Oh Lord what do I do with the great desire to praise.
The frenzied joy of detail. The fullness of

existence I feel in *contradiction*. I confess I love the
surface. The surface of all creation. Its absence of
feeling. Its presence of *sensation*. How do I stay awake
for this. The slumber is upon me. How I said to the girl
it would be all right *in the end*. Not to worry. There
                                was
another suicide here last week. One must be so careful
re the disappearance of hope. A new illusion must present
itself immediately. When I pray now
this is what I pray for. That the girl not stand like this
in the doorway, with her facts on the sheet in her right hand,
hardly able to find a normal breath. The verdict
is irreversible. Meaning the word cannot be taken back.
It is said. It is said. That is what the boy who jumped
                        left in his note.
Knocking against a stone wall says the poet
knowing the wall will not yield to any imploration. But the poet lived when there was a wall
[take away wall]. The poet lived when imploration
rose up in the human throat. When hands rose to
knock. The girl in my doorway, more terrified
by the lack of terror in the *others*—"where are all the
others" she is crying, "why does no one know, why
is this *not being reported*"—how is she supposed to bear
the silence. Someone must implore.
Someone must expect yield.
She wants the desire to cry out.
She does not want us to
go down singing. I might. She doesn't. She can be
soothed today, friend, but not tomorrow. Tomorrow she
will jump out a window or pick up a gun or believe
with a belief that hums so loudly no human reason
will ever reach into that hive again, that whatever
                        happens
will be ordained, all will be a sign,
you will never again be able to scare her,
a story so firm it will abolish the future,

coming in to grip the thing we call Time—
Don't tell her she's wrong when she comes to your
                                    doorsill.
Let her weep. Do not comfort. Do not give false
                              hope.
Tell her to tell the others. Let the dream of contagion
set loose its virus. Don't let her turn away.
I, here, today, am letting her cry out the figures, the scenarios,
am letting her wave her downloaded pages
into this normal office-air between us. 19 April. 2004.
I do not know what to tell her, Lord. I do not
                              want her
to serve you. Not you. Not you above all.

from

SEA CHANGE

(2008)

Sea Change

One day: stronger wind than anyone expected. Stronger than
                              ever before in the recording
                              of such. Un-
natural says the news. Also the body says it. Which part of the body—I look
                              down, can
                              feel it, yes, don't know
where. Also submerging us,
                              making of the fields, the trees, a cast of characters in an
                              unnegotiable
drama, ordained, iron-gloom of low light, everything at once undoing
                              itself. Also *sustained,* as in a hatred of
                              a thought, or a vanity that comes upon one out of
                              nowhere & makes
one feel the mischief in faithfulness to an
                              idea. Everything unpreventable and excited like
mornings in the unknown future. Who shall repair this now. And how the future
                              takes shape
                              too quickly. The permanent is ebbing. Is leaving
                              nothing in the way of
trails, they are blown over, grasses shoot up, life disturbing life, & it
                              fussing all over us, like a confinement gone
                              insane, blurring the feeling of
                              the state of
                              being. Which did exist just yesterday, calm and
true. Like the right to
                              privacy—how strange a feeling, here, the *right*—
                              consider your affliction says the
                              wind, do not plead ignorance, & farther and farther
                              away leaks the
past, much farther than it used to go, beating against the shutters I
                              have now fastened again, the huge mis-
                              understanding round me now so
                              still in
the center of this room, listening—oh,
                              these are not split decisions, everything

is in agreement, we set out willingly, & also knew to
play by rules, & if I say to you now
let's go

somewhere the thought won't outlast

the minute, here it is now, carrying its North
Atlantic windfall, hissing Consider
the body of the ocean which rises every instant into
me, & its
ancient e-
vaporation, & how it delivers itself

to me, how the world is our law, this indrifting of us

into us, a chorusing in us of elements, & how the
intermingling of us lacks in-
telligence, makes

reverberation, syllables untranscribable, in-clingings, & how wonder is also what

pours from us when, in the
coiling, at the very bottom of
the food
chain, sprung

from undercurrents, warming by 1 degree, the in-
dispensable

plankton is forced north now, & yet farther north,

spawning too late for the cod larvae hatch, such

that the hatch will not survive, nor the

species in the end, in the right-now forever un-
interruptible slowing of the
gulf

stream, so that I, speaking in this wind today, out loud in it, to no one, am suddenly
aware
of having written my poems, I feel it in
my useless

hands, palms in my lap, & in my listening, & also the memory of a season *at its*
full, into which is spattered like a
silly cry this in-
cessant leaf-glittering, shadow-mad, all over
the lightshafts, the walls, the bent back ranks of trees
all stippled with these slivers of

                               light like
breaking grins—infinities of them—wriggling along the walls, over the
                               grasses—mouths
                               reaching into
                               other mouths—sucking out all the
air—huge breaths passing to and fro between the unkind blurrings—& quicken
                               me further says this new wind, &
                               according to thy
                               judgment, &
I am inclining my heart towards the end,
                               I cannot fail, this Saturday, early pm, hurling myself,
wiry furies riding my many backs, against your foundations and your
                               best young
tree, which you have come outside to stake again, & the loose stones in the sill.

EMBODIES

Deep autumn & the mistake occurs, the plum tree blossoms, twelve
                              blossoms on three different
branches, which for us, personally, means none this coming spring or perhaps none on
                              just those branches on which
                              just now
lands, suddenly, a grey-gold migratory bird—still here?—crisping,
                              multiplying the wrong
                              air, shifting branches with small
hops, then stilling—very still—breathing into this oxygen which also pockets my
                              looking hard, just
                              that, takes it in, also my
                              thinking which I try to seal off,
my humanity, I was not a mistake is what my humanity thinks, I cannot
                              go somewhere
else than this body, the afterwards of each of these instants is just
                              another instant, breathe, breathe,
my cells reach out, I multiply on the face of
                              the earth, on the
mud—I can see my prints on the sweet bluish mud—where I was just
                              standing and reaching to see if
those really were blossoms, I thought perhaps paper
                              from wind, & the sadness in
me is that of forced parting, as when I loved a personal
                              love, which now seems unthinkable, & I look at
the gate, how open it is,
                              in it the very fact of God as
invention seems to sit, fast, as in its saddle, so comfortable—& where
                              does the road out of it
go—& are those torn wires hanging from the limbs—& the voice I heard once after I passed
                              what I thought was a sleeping
man, the curse muttered out, & the cage after they have let
                              the creatures
out, they are elsewhere, in one of the other rings, the ring with the empty cage is
                              gleaming, the cage is
to be looked at, grieving, for nothing, your pilgrimage ends here,

we are islands, we

should beget nothing &

what am I to do with my imagination—& the person in me trembles—& there is still

innocence, it is starting up somewhere

even now, and the strange swelling of the so-called Milky Way, and the sound of the

wings of the bird as it lifts off

suddenly, & how it is going somewhere precise, & that precision, & how I no longer

can say for sure that it

knows nothing, flaming, razory, the feathered serpent I saw as a child, of stone, &

how it stares back at me

from the height of its pyramid, & the blood flowing from the sacrifice, & the oracles

dragging hooks through the hearts in

order to say

what is coming, what is true, & all the blood, millennia, drained to stave off

the future, stave off,

& *the armies on the far plains,* the gleam off their armor now in this bird's

eye, as it flies towards me

then over, & the sound of the thousands of men assembled at

all cost now

the sound of the bird lifting, thick, rustling where it flies over—only see, it is

a hawk after all, I had not seen

clearly, it has gone to hunt in the next field, & the chlorophyll is

coursing, & the sun is

sucked in, & the chief priest walks away now where what remains of

the body is left

as is customary for the local birds.

Summer heat, the first early morning
                of it. How it lowers the pitch of the
                cry—human—cast up
as two words by the worker street-level
                positioning the long beam on
the chain as he calls up to the one handling the pulley on
                the seventh floor. One
                call. They hear each other!
Perfectly! As the dry heat, the filled-out leaves, thicken the surround, the warming
                asphalt, & the lull in growth
                occurs, & in it the single birdcries now and again
                are placed, &
all makes a round from which sound is sturdied-up without dissipation or dilation,
                bamboo-crisp, &
                up it goes up like a thing
                tossed without warp of weight or evidence of
                overcome
gravity, as if space were thinned by summer now to a non-interference. Up it goes, the
                cry, all the
                way up, audible and unchanging, so the man need
not even raise his voice to be heard,
                the dry warm air free to let it pass without
                loss of
                any of itself along
                its way…
I step out and suddenly notice this: summer arrives, has arrived, is arriving. Birds grow
                less than leaves although they cheep, dip, arc. A call
across the tall fence from an invisible neighbor to his child is heard
                right down to the secret mood in it the child
also hears. One hears in the silence that follows the great
                desire for approval
                and love
which summer holds aloft, all damp leached from it, like a thing floating out on a frail but
                perfect twig-end. Light seeming to darken in it yet
                glow. *Please* it says. But not with the eager need of

Spring! Come what may says summer. Smack in the middle I will stand and breathe. The
                              future is a superfluity I do not
                              taste, no, there is no numbering
here, it is a gorgeous swelling, no emotion, as in this love is no emotion, no, also no
                              memory—we have it all, now, & all
                              there ever was is
us, now, that man holding the beam by the right end and saying go on his
                              ground from
                              which the word and the
                              cantilevered metal
rise, there is no mistake, the right minute falls harmlessly, intimate, overcrowded,
                              without pro-
                              venance—perhaps bursting with nostalgia but
ripening so fast without growing at
                              all, & what
is the structure of freedom but this, & grace, & the politics of time—look south, look
                              north—yes—east west compile hope synthesize
exceed look look again hold fast attach speculate drift drift recognize forget—terrible
                              gush—gash—of
                              form of
outwardness, & it is your right to be so entertained, & if you are starting to
                              feel it is hunger this
                              gorgeousness, feel the heat fluctuate & say
                              my
                              name is day, of day, in day, I want nothing to
come back, not ever, & these words are mine, there is no angel to
                              wrestle, there is no inter-
                              mediary, there is something I must
tell you, you do not need existence, these words, praise be, they can for now be
                              said. That is summer. Hear them.

NEARING DAWN

Sunbreak. The sky opens its magazine. If you look hard
                    it is a process of falling
                    and squinting—& you are in-
terrupted again and again by change, & crouchings out there
                    where you are told each second you
                    are only visiting, & the secret
                    whitening adds up to no
meaning, no, not for you, wherever the loosening muscle of the night
                    startles-open the hundreds of
                    thousands of voice-boxes, into which
your listening moves like an aging dancer still trying to glide—there is time for
                    everything, everything, is there not—
                    though the balance is
                    difficult, is coming un-
done, & something strays farther from love than we ever imagined, from the long and
                    orderly sentence which was a life to us, the dry
                    leaves on
                    the fields
through which the new shoots glow
                    now also glowing, wet curled tips pointing in any
                    direction—
as if the idea of a right one were a terrible forgetting—as one feels upon
                    waking—when the dream is cutting loose, is going
                    back in the other
direction, deep inside, behind, no, just back—&
                    one is left looking out—& it is
breaking open further—what are you to do—how let it fully in—the wideness of it
                    is staggering—you have to have more arms eyes a
                    thing deeper than laughter furrows more
capacious than hate forgiveness remembrance forgetfulness history silence
                    precision miracle—more
                    furrows are needed the field
cannot be crossed this way the
                    wide shine coming towards you standing in
the open window now, a dam breaking, reeking rich with the end of

winter, fantastic weight of loam coming into the

soul, the door behind you

shut, the

great sands behind there, the pharaohs, the millennia of carefully prepared and buried

bodies, the ceremony and the weeping for them, all

back there, lamentations, libations, earth full of bodies everywhere, our bodies,

some still full of incense, & the sweet burnt

offerings, & the still-rising festival out-cryings—& we will

inherit

from it all

nothing—& our ships will still go,

after the ritual killing to make the wind listen,

out to sea as if they were going to a new place,

forgetting they must come home yet again ashamed

no matter where they have been—& always the new brides setting forth—

& always these ancient veils of theirs falling from the sky

all over us,

& my arms rising from my sides now as if in dictation, & them opening out from me,

& me now smelling the ravens the blackbirds the small heat of the rot in this largest

cage—bars of light crisping its boundaries—

& look

there is no cover, you cannot reach

it, ever, nor the scent of last night's rain, nor the chainsaw raised to take the first of the

far trees

down, nor the creek's tongued surface, nor the minnow

turned by the bottom of the current—here

is an arm outstretched, then here

is rightful day and the arm still there, outstretched, at the edge of a world—tyrants

imagined by the bearer of the arm, winds listened for,

corpses easily placed anywhere the

mind wishes—inbox, outbox—machines

that do not tire in the

distance—barbed wire taking daysheen on—marking the end of the field—the barbs like a

lineup drinking itself

crazy—the wire

where it is turned round the post standing in for

mental distress—the posts as they start down the next field sorting his from

                         mine, his from the
                         other's—until you know, following,
following, all the way to the edge and then turning again, then again, to the
                         far fields, to the
height of the light—you know
                         you have no destiny, no, you have a wild unstoppable
                         rumor for a soul, you
look all the way to the end of
                         your gaze, why did you marry, why did you stop to listen,
where are your fingerprints, the mud out there hurrying to
                         the white wood gate, its ruts, the ants in it, your
                         imagination of your naked foot placed
there, the thought that in that there
                         is all you have & that you have
no rightful way
                         to live—

Day Off

from the cadaver beginning to show through the skin of the day. The future without
days. Without days of it?
in it? I try to—just for a second—feel
that shape. What weeds-up out of nowhere as you look away for
good. So that you have to imagine
whatever's growing there growing forever. You shall not be back to look
again. The last glance like a footprint before the
thing it was
takes flight. Disturbing nothing, though,
as it is
nothing. Air moving aside air. That breeze. How is this possible, yet it
must be. Otherwise it cannot be said that this
existed. Or that we did, today. Always breathing-in this pre-life, exhaling this post.
Something goes away, something comes
back. But through you. Leaving no trail but self. As trails go not much of
one. But patiently
you travel it. Your self. You hardly disturb anything actually, isn't it strange. For all
the fuss of *being* how little
you disturb. Also like
a seam, this trail. Something is being
repaired. No? Yes. Push *save*. Write your name again to register. It is some
bride, this flesh barely hanging
on, of minutes, of minutiae, of whatever it is
raising now
up through day's skin as a glance, a toss of hand, in conversation, as, growing in-
creasingly unburied now, one can begin to see
the speechless toil, there under day's department, under the texture of
keeping-on-
doing-it, whatever it is that has variation in it, that swallows clip, that the
trellis of minutes holds letting clouds slip
through if you
look up—it seems we are
fresh out of ideas—the pre-war life disappeared, just like that, don't look back you'll
get stiff-necked—there is exhaust in the air in its

place—the wilderness (try to think of it) does nothing but point to here, how we
                                      got here, says it can't stay
                                      a minute longer
                                      but that we
                                      will have to—& day
something I am feeling lean on my shoulders now, & how
                                      free it is, this day, how it seems to bend its
                                      long neck
over me and try to peer at me, right here, right into my face—how it is so worried in
                                      its hollowing-out over me—night in it starting to
trickle down, & the sensation of punishment though still far away, horns in the
                                      distance, & how this was a schooling, & plain
truths which shine out like night-bugs in evening, no one can catch them as
                                      they blink
                                      and waft, & that summer will be here
soon, which is normal, which we notice is normal, & will our fear matter to
                                      anything is a thing we
                                      wonder, & before you know it
we are ready to begin thinking about something else,
                                      while behind us it is approaching at
                                      last the day of
days, where all you have named is finally shunted aside, the whole material man-
                                      ifestation of so-called definitions, imagine
that, the path of least resistance wherein I grab onto the immaterial and christen it
                                      thus and thus &
something over our shoulders says it is good, yes, go on, go on, and we did.

ROOT END

The desire to imagine

 the future.

 Walking in the dark through a house you know by

heart. Calm. Knowing no one will be

 out there.

 Amazing

 how you can move among

 the underworld's

 furniture—

the walls glide by, the desks, here a mirror sends back an almost unseeable

 blink—a faraway lighthouse,

 moonlessness—a planet going

 out—here a

knotting of yet greater dark suggests

 a door—a hollow feeling is a stair—the difference between

 up and down a differential—so slight—of

 temperature

 and shift of provenance of

 void—the side of your face

reads it—as if one could almost overhear laughter "down" there, birdcall "up" there—

 although this is only an

 analogy for different

 silences—oh—

 the mind knows our place so

deeply well—you could run through it—without fear—even in this total dark—this is what

 the mind says in you: accelerate!—it is your

 place, you be-

 long, you know it by

 heart, place—

 not imaginable, nor under-

 stood, where death is still an in-

dividual thing, & in the dark outside only the garden, & in each plant at core a thing

 by

heart, & *after all these years* the heart says to itself each

 beat, & look, if you make yourself think of it,

                              the roads out there will branch and branch then
                              vanish,
fanning out, flat, thinning away like root-ends, everywhere going only forward—&
                              so far from any so-called
                              city on the
hill, this city of dis-

                              appearance, root-ends then nothing, thinnest trailings of
                              all, forgiveness says the dark, smell
me breathe me in I am your inheritance forgive it,
                              dusk is already crushed tight and cannot be looked into
anymore, the glance between hunter and prey is choked off, under the big tent the
                              numbered rows grew
                              numberless long
                              ago, admittance is
                              free, as in you have
no choice, we are trying to block out the sound of drums in the distance, blessed be his
                              name says someone far in front at the
                              mike, & seats numbered 1 through 6 billion are
                              reserved, &
                              the story of the parted lovers, the one from the prior order,
will begin soon, you will see through the dark to it as it will
                              light itself
                              of its own accord,
also moonlight, what can filter through of it—&
                              look hard for where they rise and act, look hard to see
                              what action was—fine strength—it turns one inside out—
                              what is this growing inside of me, using me—such that the
wind can no longer blow through me—such that the dream in me grows cellular, then
                              muscular, my eyes red, my birth a thing I convey
                              beautifully
down this spiral staircase
                              made of words, made of
nothing but words—

THE VIOLINIST AT THE WINDOW, 1918

(after Matisse)

Here he is again, so thin, unbent, one would say captive—did winter ever leave—no one
has climbed the hill north of town in longer than one can remember—something hasn't
been fully loaded—life is blameless—he is a stem—& what here is cyclic, we would so
                              need to know
                              about now—& if there is
                              a top to this—a summit, the highest note, a
                              destination—
here he is now, again, standing at the window, ready to
                              look out if asked to
                              by his
                              time,
                              ready to take up again if he
                              must, here where the war to end all wars has come
                              to an end—for a while—to take up whatever it is
                              the spirit
must take up, & what is the melody of
                              that, the sustained one note of obligatory
                              hope, taken in, like a virus,
                              before the body grows accustomed to it and it
                              becomes
                              natural again—yes breathe it in,
                              the interlude,
                              the lull in the
                              killing—up
                              the heart is asked to go, up—
open these heavy shutters now, the hidden order of a belief system
                              trickles to the fore,
                              it insists you draw closer to
                              the railing—lean out—
time stands out there as if mature, blooming, big as day—& is this not an emaciated
                              sky, & how
                              thin is this
                              sensation of time, do you
not feel it, the no in the heart—no, do not make me believe

again, too much has died, do not make me open this
all up
again—crouching in
shadow, my head totally
empty—you can see
the whole sky pass through this head of mine, the mind is hatched and scored by clouds
and weather—what is weather—when it's
all gone we'll
buy more,
heaven conserve us is the song, & lakes full of leaping
fish, & ages that shall not end, dew-drenched, sun-
drenched, price-
less—leave us alone, loose and undone, everything
and nothing slipping through—no, I cannot be reached, I cannot be duped again says
my head standing now in the
opened-up window, while history starts up again, &
is that flute music in the
distance, is that an answering machine—call and response—& is that ringing in my ears
the furrows of earth
full of men and their parts, & blood as it sinks into
loam, into the page of statistics, & the streets out there, shall we really
be made to lay them out again, & my plagiarized
humanity, whom
shall I now imitate to re-
become
before the next catastrophe—the law of falling bodies applies but we shall not use
it—the law of lateness—
even our loved ones don't know if we're living—
but I pick it up again, the
violin, it is
still here
in my left hand, it has been tied to me all this long time—I shall hold it, my
one burden, I shall hear the difference between up
and
down, & up we shall bring the bow now up &
down, & find
the note, sustained, fixed, this is what hope forced upon oneself by one's self sounds

124

like—this high note trembling—it is a
good sound, it is an
ugly sound, my hand is doing this, my mind cannot
open—cloud against sky, the freeing of my self
from myself, the note is that, I am standing in
my window, my species is ill, the
end of the world can be imagined, minutes run away like the pattering of feet in summer
down the long hall then out—oh be happy, &
clouds roil, & they hide the slaughterhouse, they loft as if this were
not
perpetual exile—we go closer—the hands at the end of this body
feel in their palms
the great
desire—look—the instrument is raised—
& this will be a time again in which to *make*—a time of uselessness—the imagined human
paradise.

FUTURES

Midwinter. Dead of. I own you says my mind. Own what, own
                              whom. I look up. Own the looking at us
say the cuttlefish branchings, lichen-black, moist. Also
                              the seeing, which wants to feel more than it sees.
Also, in the glance, the feeling of owning, accordioning out and up,
                              seafanning,
& there is cloud on blue ground up there, & wind which the eye loves so deeply it
                              would spill itself out and liquefy
                              to pay for it—
& the push of owning is thrilling, is spring before it
                              is—is that swelling—is the imagined fragrance as one
bends, before the thing is close enough—wide-
                              eyed leaning—although none of this can make you
                              happy—
because, looking up, the sky makes you hear it, you know why we have come it
                              blues, you know the trouble at the heart, blue, blue, what
pandemonium, blur of spears roots cries leaves master & slave, the crop destroyed,
                              water everywhere not
                              drinkable, & radioactive waste in it, & human bodily
waste, & what,
                              says the eye-thinking heart, is the last color seen, the last word
heard—someone left behind, then no behind—
                              is there a skin of the I own which can be scoured from inside the
                              glance—no,
                              cannot—& always
                              someone walking by whistling a
                              little tune, that's
life he says, smiling, there, that was life—& the heart branches with its
                              wild arteries—I own my self, I own my
leaving—the falcon watching from the tree—I shall torch the crop that no one else
                              have it whispers the air—
& someone's swinging from a rope, his rope—the eye
                              throbbing—day a noose looking for a neck—
the fire spidery but fast—& the idea of
                              friends, what was that, & the day, in winter, your lower back

started acting up again, & they pluck out the eyes at the end for

food, & don't forget

the meeting at 6, your child's teacher

wishes to speak to you

about his future, & if there is no food and the rain is everywhere switching-on as expected,

& you try to think of music and the blue of Giotto,

& if they have to eat the arms he will feel no pain at least, & there is a

sequence in which feeding takes

place—the body is owned by the hungry—one is waiting

one's turn—one wants to own one's

turn—and standing there,

don't do it now but you might remember kisses—how you kissed his arm in the sun

and

tasted the sun, & this is your

address now, your home address—& the strings are cut no one

looks up any longer

—or out—no—&

one day a swan appeared out of nowhere on the drying river,

it

was sick, but it floated, and the eye felt the pain of rising to take it in—I own you

said the old feeling, I want

to begin counting

again, I will count what is mine, it is moving quickly now, I will begin this

message "I"—I feel the

smile, put my hand up to be sure, yes on my lips—the yes—I touch it again, I

begin counting, I say *one* to the swan, *one,*

do not be angry with me o my god, I have begun the action of beauty again, on

the burning river I have started the catalogue,

your world,

I your speck tremble remembering money, its dry touch, sweet strange

smell, it's a long time, the smell of it like lily of the valley

sometimes, and pondwater, and how

one could bend down close to it

and drink.

UNDATED LULLABY

I go out and there she is still of course sitting on the nest, dead-center in-
                              visible in our flowing big-
                              headed
still young and staked acacia, crown an almost
                              perfect
                              circle, dark greens blurring now
in this high wind, wrestling it, compliant too—billion-mouthed transformer of
                              sun and the carbon molecule—
                              & you have to stand still and
                              look in to see her,
there where the wind splits open the head, slashes the branches, & you see her,
                              & her head does not even turn or
                              tuck—
heart, jewel, bloom, star—not on any rung as we are on rungs—I can't help but
                              look,
                              wind-slicings keep
                              revealing her, felt-still, absorbent of
light, sound, gaze, idea—I have seen everything bought and sold I think—
                              the human heart is a
                              refugee—is standing here always in
                              its open
                              market, shouting out prices, in-
audible prices, & wares keep on arriving, & the voices get higher—
                              what are you worth the map of the world is
shrieking, any moment of you, what is it
                              worth, time breaks over you and you
                              remain, more of you, more of you,
asking your questions, ravishing the visible with your inquiry, and hungry, why are you
                              so hungry, you have already been
                              fed, close your
mouth, close your neck, close your hands chest mind, close them—& your eyes,
                              close them—make arrangements to hold
                              yourself together, that will be needed, make of your
                              compassion a
crisper instrument, you will need its blade, you will need

128

bitterness, stand here all you like looking in, you
will need to learn
to live in this prison
of blood and breath,
& the breeze passes by so generously, & the air
has the whole earth in its mind and it thinks it, thinks it, & in the corner of your cell
look carefully, you are of the ones who worship
cruelty—looking in to her nest, the bloom which is your heart opens with
kindness,
you can feel it flow through you as your eyes take her
in—strange sweetness this—high note—held—
but it is in your hands you must look
for the feeling of what is human,
and in your palms feel
what the tall clouds on the horizon oar-in to you—what will forever replace
stillness of mind—
look out for them their armada is not aware of your air-conditioned
office—swimmingly the thunderheads arrive &
when
is the last time you cried out loud, & who are those there
still shuffling through their files,
trying to card-out what to shred
in time, &
are you still giving out character references, to
whom, & the tickets, who paid for them this
time—your
voice, was it raised too high for the
circumstance—were you too
visible,
did you make sufficient progress, is the address still in your pocket, who paid, who left
the tip, the garden, the
love, the thirst—oh who
was so hungry they ate of the heaven, they ate the piece of it, they ripped its
seam—look the stitching is coming
undone—moon, river-in-the
distance, stars above the tree, wind dying down—why are you
still here—the end of evening has *come*

and gone—crammed to its full with the whole garden and its creatures—why
                              are you still here, your eyes like mouths—shut them now—&
                              tuck in your pleasure, tuck it in,
move on into the deeper water, your kind
                              await you, sprawling in their camps,
                              longing to be recognized,
& the harsh priest the cold does his nightly round,
                              & the huge flower of reason blooms, blooms,
& somebody has a newspaper, not today's, no, but some day's,
                              and if you can find a corner,
you can pick it up—ignoring the squint-eyed girl, the sensation of
                              falling, the general theory of
relativity, the nest of
                              meaning—you can sit in your exile
and, to the tune of the latest song, the recording of what was at some moment the song
                              of the moment, the *it* song, the thing
                              you couldn't
miss—it was everywhere—everyone was singing it—you can find your
                              mind
                              and in the firelight
catch up on that distant moment's news.

No Long Way Round

Evening. Not quite. High winds again.
                              I have time, my time, as you also do, there, feel
                              it. And a heart, my heart, as you do,
remember it. Also am sure of some things, there are errands, this was a voyage, one
                              has an ordained part to play....This will turn out to be
                              not true
but is operative here for me this evening as the dusk settles. One has to believe
                              furthermore in the voyage of others. The dark
                              gathers. It is advancing but there is no
progress. It is advancing with its bellyful of minutes. It seems to chew as it
                              darkens. There was, in such a time, in addition,
an obligation to what we called telling
                              the truth. We
                              liked
                              the feeling
                              of it—truth—whatever we meant by it—I can still
feel it in my gaze, tonight, long after it is gone, that finding of all the fine discriminations,
                              the edges, purse holding the goods, snap shut, there,
you got it, there, it is yours it is true—hold onto it as
                              light thins
                              holding the lavender in its heart, firm, slow, beginning to
hide it, to steal it, to pretend it never had
                              existence. At the window, I stand spell-
bound. Your excellency the evening, I begin. What is this trickiness. I am passing
                              through your checkpoint to a nation that is
disappearing, is disappearance. My high-ceilinged room (I look
                              up) is only going to survive
                              invisibility
                              for the while longer we
                              have the means
to keep it. I look at the pools of light in it. The carpet shining-up its weave—
burgundy, gold, aqua, black. It is an emergency actually, this waking and doing and
cleaning-up afterwards, & then sleep again, & then up you go, the whole 15,000 years of
the inter-
                              glacial period, & the orders & the getting done &

the getting back in time & the turning it back on, & did you remember, did you pass, did
you lose the address again, didn't the machine spit it up, did you follow the machine—
yes, yes, did, & the

                                    wall behind it

                                    pronounced the large bush then took it

back. I can almost summon it. Like changing a tense. I peer back through this time to

                                    that one. You will not believe it

                                    when the time

comes. Also how we mourned our dead—had

                                    ample earth, took time, opened it, closed

                                    it—"our earth, our

                                    dead" we called

                                    them, & lived

bereavement, & had strict understandings of defeat and victory.... Evening,

                                    what are the betrayals that are left,

                                    and whose? I ask now

as the sensation of what is coming places its shoulders on the whole horizon, I see it

                                    though it is headless, intent

                                    fuzzy, possible outcomes

unimaginable. You have your imagination, says the evening. It is all you have

                                    left, but its neck is open, the throat is

cut, you have not forgotten how to sing, or to want

                                    to sing. It is

                                    strange but you still

                                    need to tell

your story—how you met, the coat one wore, the shadow of which war, and how it lifted,

                                    and how peace began again

                                    for that part of

the planet, & the first Spring after your war, & how "life" began again, what

                                    normal was—thousands of times

                                    you want to say this—normal—holding another's

hand—& the poplars when you saw how much they had grown while you were

                                    away—

                                    the height of them! & the paper lantern you were

                                    given to hold—the lightness of it, of its

fire, how it lit the room—it was your room—you were alone in it and free to sleep

                                    without worry and to

dream—winter outside and the embroidered tablecloth—fruit and water—you didn't
even wonder where was the tree that gave such fruit, you lay in blankets as if they were
non-existent, heat was a given, the rain coming down hard now, what a nice sound—you
could ruminate, the mind traveled back in those days, at ease, it recalled the evening's
con-
                              versation, the light that fell on x's face, how he
turned when a certain person entered the room—you saw him turn—saw shyness then
jealousy enter his eyes as he looked away—and did he see you see him—and the embroidered linen handkerchief you saw a frightened woman in the subway slide from her
pocket, use and replace—then sleep was near—somewhere you were a child and then this
now, nightfall and ease, hospitality—
                              there are sounds the planet will always make, even
if there is no one to hear them.

NOTES

Poems from *The Errancy*

'The Guardian Angel of the Little Utopia'
Five lines from the end, the line is from Henry Vaughan's 'Distraction'.

'That Greater Than Which Nothing'
Near the end, the phrase 'it's the light, you can't keep it out' is from Charles Wright's poem 'Virgo Descending'.

'Le Manteau de Pascal'
All the 'Manteau' poems in *The Errancy* are loosely inspired by the Magritte painting of Pascal's coat. One presumes it represents the coat in which Pascal was buried, and in whose hem or sleeve or 'fold' the note containing 'the irrefutable proof of the existence of God' is said to have been stitched, at his request, by his sister, upon his death. The section dated 'July 11' is a fragment from Hopkins' journals. In section 13 the quotations are from Magritte's notebooks.

Poems from *Swarm*

from 'The Reformation Journal'
The first three lines use fragments from Gunnar Ekelof. The phrases in quotation marks are from Thomas Traherne and Emily Dickinson respectively.

'Middle Distance'
The first phrase in quotation marks is from David Jones, the second from Susan Howe.

'Prayer (after Hölderlin)'
The poem is built in great part of fragments from his long poems *Dichterberuf* ('The Poet's Vocation'), and *Stimme des Volks* ('Voice of the People'), in the Christopher Middleton translation.

from 'The Reformation Journal (2)'
The phrase in quotation marks which constitutes the next-to-last stanza is from Plato's *Phaedo* and refers to the death of Socrates.

Poems from *Never*

'Prayer'
This was written as a turn-of-the-millennium poem for the *New York Times* Op-Ed page, and was originally dated 12.31.00.

'Evolution' [How old are you?]
Some of the questions were provided by the questionnaire the *New York Times* used in conducting the poll the results of which were given me as an 'assignment' for this poem. An additional fact, which reached me while I was writing the poem, struck me: during the 1850s, while Darwin was concluding *On the Origin of Species*, the rate of extinction (for species) is believed to have been one every five years. Today, the rate of extinction is estimated at one every nine minutes. Throughout the writing of this book, I was haunted by the sensation of that nine-minute span – which might amount to the time it takes to read any poem here before you. My sense of that time frame (and its inevitable increase, even as we 'speak') inhabits, as well as structures, the book [*Never*]. It is written up against the sensation of what is now called 'ecocide'. I was also influenced by, among other texts, the 'World Scientists' Warning to Humanity', sponsored by the Union of Concerned Scientists (1993).

Poems from *Overlord*

In November 1943 Stalin, Churchill and Roosevelt met in Tehran and agreed the Allies would mount a major offensive, opening a second front, in Europe. General Eisenhower was put in charge of what became known as 'Operation Overlord', which included the landing on Omaha Beach, in the Normandy region of France, on what came to be known as D-Day: 6 June 1944. It is customary for the military to denote days prior to, and after, that day with a plus or minus sign, as well as designating the scheduled hour of the invasion as H Hour.

'Soldatenfriedhof'
This is a literal account. My thanks to Lucien Tisserand, Conservateur of the German Military Cemetery at La Cambe. I am much indebted, as well, to the spirit of *Les Jardins de la Mémoire*, by Annick Helias (with Françoise Avril, Dominique Bassiere, Paul Colin and Patrick Galineau), for leading me to an on-site study of the military graveyards in Normandy.

'Praying (Attempt of May 9, '03)'
A different version of this poem first appeared under the title 'Third' in the book *Bits & Pieces Put Together to Present a Semblance of a Whole* on the permanent collection of the Walker Art Museum. In

an early reworking, the poem became a meditation on Barnett Newman's painting *The Third* (1962).

'Spoken from the Hedgerows'
Voices here are accurately named, and their trajectories towards the staging grounds for Operation Overlord in Britain are also accurate, although condensed, as recounted in *Voices of D-Day*, edited by Ronald J. Drez (Louisiana State University Press, 1994). By May 1944, almost 1,500,000 fighting men were bivouacked in Great Britain while awaiting action.